Introducing

Black Theology

3 Crucial Questions
Grant R. Osborne, editor

Introducing
Black Theology

3 Crucial Questions for the Evangelical Church

Bruce L. Fields

Baker Academic
A Division of Baker Book House Co
Grand Rapids, Michigan 49516

Published by Baker Academic
a division of Baker Book House Company
P.O. Box 6287, Grand Rapids, MI 49516–6287

Printed in the United States of America

Library of Congress Cataloging-in-Publication Data

Fields, Bruce L., 1951–
    Introducing Black theology : 3 crucial questions for the
Evangelical Church / Bruce L. Fields.
        p.   cm. — (3 crucial questions)
    Includes bibliographical references and index.
    ISBN 0-8010-2278-9
    1. Black theology. I. Title. II. Series.
BT82.7.F54   2001
230′.089′96073—dc21   00-068062

For information about academic books, resources for Christian leaders, and all new releases available from Baker Book House, visit our web site:
http://www.bakerbooks.com

To my wife, Mary,
and our children,
Caleb, Michael, Rebekah, and Rachel;
marvelous manifestations of the grace,
mercy, and love of the Lord.

Contents

Editor's Preface

The 3 Crucial Questions series is based on two fundamental observations. First, there are crucial questions related to the Christian faith for which imperfect Christians seem to have no final answers. Christians living in eternal glory may know fully even as they are known by God, but now we know only in part (1 Cor. 13:12). Therefore, we must ever return to such questions with the prayer that God the Holy Spirit will continue to lead us nearer to "the truth, the whole truth, and nothing but the truth." While recognizing their own frailty, the authors contributing to this series pray that they are thus led.

Second, each Christian generation partly affirms its solidarity with the Christian past by reaffirming "the faith which was once delivered unto the saints" (Jude 3 KJV). Such an affirmation is usually attempted by religious scholars who are notorious for talking only to themselves or by nonexperts whose grasp of the faith lacks depth of insight. Both situations are unfortunate, but we feel that our team of contributing authors is well prepared to avoid them. Each author is a competent, Christian scholar able to share tremendous learning in down-to-earth language both laity and experts can appreciate. In a word, you have in hand a book that is part of a rare series—one that is neither pedantic nor pediatric.

The topics addressed in the series have been chosen for their timelessness, interest level, and importance to Christians everywhere, and the contributing authors are committed to discussing them in a manner that promotes Christian unity. Thus, the authors discuss not only areas of disagreement among Christians but significant areas of agreement as well. Seeking peace and pursuing it as the Bible commands (1 Peter 3:11), they stress common ground on which Christians with different views may meet for wholesome dialogue and reconciliation.

The books in the series consist not merely of printed words; they consist of words by which to live. Their pages are filled not only with good information but with sound instruction in successful Christian living. For study is truly Christian only when, in addition to helping us understand our faith, it helps us to live our faith. I pray, therefore, that you will allow God to use the 3 Crucial Questions series to augment your growth in the grace and knowledge of our Lord and Savior Jesus Christ.

Grant R. Osborne

1
What Is Black Theology?

What is black theology? Isn't there just "theology"? Is it really necessary to speak of "black theology," and even if we do, should we then speak of "Asian theology," "Native American theology," and so forth?" These are the types of questions I have heard countless times during both my seminary years as a student and my professional teaching ministry.

Those who ask these questions often make several assumptions. First, they think that social, cultural, and religious factors do not affect theological formulation. Many do not understand that the formulation of doctrine, the exploration of the relationships between doctrines, and the commitment to applying theology to life can lead to different emphases. Second, they assume that racial factors with accompanying sociocultural elements do not and should not influence the development of theology. Third, members of these particular communities believe they already have the theology needed for the edification of the church.[1]

The issue of the legitimacy and contributions of black theology is not one that can be ignored in theological discourse. The history of the church in the United States includes varied responses and reactions to the issues of race. The way theological convictions have been expressed and applied have reflected racial preferences at various times and in various places throughout our history. I will discuss some specific examples later in this chapter. My purpose here is to introduce the fact that sociohistorical factors in the church have contributed to the development of black theology, which is a theological response, at least in its early forms, to racism.

An impartial evaluation of the nature and purpose of black theology is possible only if the proponents of black theology are heard on their own terms. What is needed is a sincere engagement with the discipline, and thus my discussion will be somewhat sympathetic. Although I disagree with much in black theology, there is much that I believe is valid, particularly in its criticisms of Christianity as historically and presently practiced.

In this chapter I will present a definition of black theology, as well as the sources, hermeneutics, and task of the black theologian. I will discuss these areas in light of the thought of some widely recognized foundational theologians in the discipline. Some members of the second generation of black theologians will be mentioned in the course of this study, but the majority of material will be from the first generation. The remaining two chapters flesh out some implications from this discussion on the nature of black theology. In the second chapter I will offer some thoughts on what black theology can teach the conservative evangelical church. Black theology brings some needed reminders and points of confrontation to the theological table. The third chapter will be made up of personal reflections on the future of black theology. Within black theology there are many topics worthy of more in-depth treatment. I cannot regularly achieve this, but my hope is that I will spur the reader on to further investigation.

Definition of Black Theology

The following definition contributes much toward an understanding of black theology. It comes from a statement by the National Committee of Black Churchmen in 1969:

> Black Theology is a theology of black liberation. It seeks to plumb the black condition in the light of God's revelation in Jesus Christ, so that the black community can see that the gospel is commensurate with the achievement of black humanity. Black Theology is a theology of "blackness." It is the affirmation of black humanity that emancipates black people from white racism, thus providing authentic freedom for both white and black people. It affirms the humanity of white people in that it says No to the encroachment of white oppression.[2]

In light of the depth of thought and intensity of expression evident in this statement, some explication is appropriate.

Without question the goal of liberation governs the theological formulation of black theology. James Cone defines liberation as the struggle for "political, social, and economic justice."[3] J. Deotis Roberts sees liberation as the theme of black theology: "Christ is the liberator and the Christian faith promises 'deliverance to the captives.' It promises to let the oppressed go free."[4] Cone and Roberts address concerns of liberation against the backdrop of the reality of racism and its manifestations in social, political, and religious realms. In more recent years, the parameters of oppression as addressed in black theology have been extended to encompass not only racism, but sexism and what some consider to be homophobia.[5]

Black theology seeks to make sense of the sociohistorical experience of African-Americans[6] in light of their confession that God has given revelation in Jesus Christ. This revelatory act makes possible the conviction that the struggle for justice is consistent with the gospel.[7]

"Blackness" is not just a reference to skin color;[8] it is a symbol abounding in meaning and force. The reality of rejection, dehumanization, fear, and oppression is reflected in this word. As a symbol of oppression, the concept of blackness allows for fruitful theological reflection. Cone argues that God is black in that "God has made the oppressed condition his own condition."[9] Similarly, Jesus is black because he identifies with a community that is oppressed because of its blackness.[10] Blackness is that which all oppressed people share in solidarity both with each other and with the God who is on the side of the oppressed.[11]

Blackness is not only a symbol of oppression and the solidarity of the oppressed community with God, but it also symbolizes the movement to ascribe worth to black life in America.[12] When I was a young child during the 1950s, calling a Negro "black" was considered an insult. With the rise of the black power movement of the 1960s, being black became a symbol of pride, a reason to hold one's head up high. Blackness affirmed that "black is beautiful" and renewed an appreciation for other unique institutions and practices of African-American life.[13] It inspired a thirst for knowledge about the roots of the African-American heritage on the African continent. It inspired an embracing of this heritage.

An affirmation of blackness did not call for hatred of whiteness; rather, the emphasis was on affirming all that African-Americans had been taught to reject and despise about themselves.[14] Affirmation of personhood contributed to the motivation and agenda for freedom from systemic racism. Indeed, saying no to white oppression was an affirming of the humanity of white people. By saying no to oppression, the African-American community might aid in the process of liberating the white community. Whites could be humanized through surrendering their assumptions of superiority and their oppressive institutionalized practices that perpetuated their false self-understanding.[15] The Brazilian educator Paulo Freire argued for this interpretation of the liberative process:

> This, then, is the great humanistic and historical task of the oppressed: to liberate themselves and their oppressors as well. The oppressors, who oppress, exploit, and rape by virtue of

their power, cannot find in this power the strength to liberate either the oppressed or themselves.[16]

By implication, then, African-Americans could no longer yield to white oppression because in doing so they would deny their own humanity and that of white people as well.

Black theology involves the process of formulating theology from the perspective of an oppressed people. It seeks to interpret the gospel of Jesus Christ against the backdrop of historical and contemporary racism. The message of black theology is that the African-American struggle for liberation is consistent with the gospel. Every theological statement must be consistent with the goals of liberation and perpetuate those goals.

Liberation is the goal for African-Americans and for whites because both exist in the sphere of oppression. Whites would be freed from their misinformed view of superiority to understand anew that all human beings are made in the image of God. When whites deny or undermine this reality, they are enslaved because they are ruled by a perspective other than the Creator's. As liberation relates to the African-American community, it involves not only social, political, and economic empowerment. It also demands the right of self-definition, self-affirmation, and self-determination for the African-American community. Black theology provides the theological legitimacy for such a process. The telos of black theology thus shares many of the objectives of liberation and feminist theology. The black experience, however, is the point of departure from these other disciplines. I will address the matter of the black experience below.

The Sources of Black Theology

Cone argues that black theologians cannot formulate theology in a realm unrelated to human existence. Therefore, black theology must emerge from the historical and religious experience of African-American people. Cone sees what he calls the "black experience" as the first source of black theology.[17]

There are a number of aspects that make up the black experience, including the stories, tales, and sayings of African-Americans that have developed as they have endured existence in a racist society. These expressions of life may be in the form of songs, poems, narratives, and music.[18] The black experience is about uncovering reasons to affirm African-American personhood, culture, and values when much in the surrounding sociocultural setting undervalues such manifestations. These positive affirmations contribute to the development of communal structures that keep the members of the community from despair and inactivity.[19]

Black history contributes to an explication of the black experience, but it makes another unique contribution in the framing of a liberating theology. Specifically, it provides a theater where the liberating activities of God can be observed. Cone synthesized biblical testimony and black history when he wrote,

> In Jesus' death and resurrection, God has freed us to fight against social and political structures while not being determined by them. . . . God is the sovereign ruler and nothing can thwart his will to liberate the oppressed.[20]

Biblical history, through events of liberation such as the exodus, confirms that God acts on behalf of the oppressed. God has shown such intervention in black history by providing hope for continued works of liberation.

A focal point of God's historical liberating activity was and is the black church. The black church was not only the place where these oppressed people could be affirmed in their personal worth, but there they also heard stories and sermons about the Lord who was always at work. They would be strengthened through the personal sharing of those who would say, "God is a heart-fixer and a mind-regulator. He is the One who binds the broken heart and eases the pain of the afflicted. He rescued me from the gates of hell and restored my soul to his bosom."[21] The black church historically has empowered African-Americans to a ministry that met spiritual and material needs.[22] It has consistently provided strong models for the struggle against racist oppression. The black church has a long and influential history dating back to the days of slavery.

Gayraud Wilmore observes that the Mother Bethel African Methodist Episcopal Church began as a protest against the blatant segregation of St. George's Methodist Episcopal Church in Philadelphia.[23] The founder of this new wing of the Methodist church was Richard Allen. Lester Scherer reports how events reached a climax in 1787 when the white congregation refused to sanction the formation of an independent black congregation. During a prayer meeting,

> Allen, Absalom Jones, and other blacks were apparently confused as to which seats in a new gallery they were expected to occupy. They took the "wrong" ones with the result that a white trustee pulled Jones to his feet during prayer in an effort to make him change seats. The whole black group walked out of the service and soon formed the Free African Society, which was organized under a church-like discipline and became for a while an independent African Church.[24]

Wilmore points out that Allen, nevertheless, later chose to remain in the Methodist tradition.[25]

The historic black church provided other models of an admittedly more militant nature in those who contemplated a more direct relationship between the stories and teaching of the Bible, particularly the Old Testament, and the slaves' struggle for freedom. Other factors influenced these more militant figures. Wilmore identified things such as "a deeply-lying African spirituality, a kind of God-madness, an enthusiasm for dream interpretation, visions, and prophecy."[26] These factors, working in conjunction with the stories of

Israel's deliverance from Egypt and from other enemies, produced a paradigm by which they understood that God acts to bring freedom to enslaved peoples. Enlightened clergy and laypeople derived inspiration and found powerful imagery for fiery prophetic messages against slavery in the biblical tradition, though it did not necessarily result in armed violence. Such people included Robert Alexander Young and David Walker.[27]

Some who united biblical imagery and teaching with active rebellion against slavery were men like Gabriel Prosser, Denmark Vesey, and Nat Turner, who Wilmore labeled the "Three Generals in the Lord's Army."[28] Prosser saw himself as the black Samson sent by God to deliver his people from slavery. He was going to lead a slave army on Richmond, Virginia, to capture arms from the arsenal, loot the treasury, and if possible, make an agreement with slave owners for the release of those who remained in slavery. A great storm prevented his planned attack on August 30, 1800. Soon after this, Prosser was betrayed, captured, and executed on October 7, 1800.[29] Fear spread throughout Virginia when authorities made known the details of the derailed rebellion.

In the year that Gabriel Prosser was executed, Denmark Vesey won a lottery and purchased his freedom from Captain Joseph Vesey. He led a slave insurrection in Charleston, South Carolina, twenty-two years after obtaining his freedom. Like Prosser, Vesey was engrossed in the study of the Bible, although he engaged in the admittedly questionable interpretation of passages such as Zechariah 14 and Joshua 6 to justify his militance. The successful slave revolt led by Toussaint L'Ouverture in Haiti (begun in 1791) served as an inspiration for Vesey and his lieutenants.[30] One of Vesey's inner circle had written to the president of Haiti informing him of an imminent rebellion.[31] The date of the attack was Sunday, June 16, but it was thwarted through betrayal. Vesey and some of his lieutenants were eventually captured and executed on July 2, 1822.

Inspired by Vesey's near success, other insurrections followed in various parts of the state, but they were often brutally suppressed. Wholesale executions in South Carolina helped fan the flames of the antislavery movement, particularly in the North. Wilmore observes that black Christians continued to believe that God had aligned himself with them in their struggle:

> They came to the conclusion that after the blood of their martyrs had soaked the red clay of Dixie, many whites—in a tragic and cataclysmic struggle—would pay with their own lives for the blasphemy of holding in chains other human beings created in God's image.[32]

Nat Turner was a Baptist preacher who joined the membership of these generals in the Lord's army by leading a revolt in Southampton, Virginia, in the summer of 1831.[33] Many people among Turner's peers anticipated even from his early years that he was going to be a preacher. He used to spend long periods of time in meditation and prayer. Luke 12:35–51 was a pivotal passage to Turner because it convinced him that true freedom and peace would come only through the sword. When Thomas R. Gray asked Turner how he arrived at such an interpretation of this passage, he pointed out what he saw as the connection between Jesus of Nazareth and the prophets who cried out to God for judgment on a disobedient people.[34] After Turner and his men massacred a number of whites, he was eventually captured on October 30, 1831, and was hanged two weeks later.

Wilmore's generals provide models for contemporary black theological reflection. They all shared a deep hatred of slavery. Each relied upon his interpretation of Scripture for vision and for understanding what he believed he was divinely required to be and do in the struggle for freedom. They shared a conviction that God has been, is, and will always be involved in bringing freedom to oppressed people. Even Jesus, "meek and mild," was a prophet proclaiming God's will for justice. These men believed these things from the depths of their souls, their deaths giving clear testimony to the intensity and unwavering commitment to their convictions. Such people provided inspiration for liberation-oriented black theologians, both male and female.

It should not be surprising that black history, a history built upon and permeated by the black church, also provided female prophets as models for liberation. Bennett suggests that the most renowned of the female abolitionists were Harriet Tubman and Sojourner Truth, "who created the twin mountain peaks of the heroic tradition of black women."[35] Both women were dramatically affected by religious beliefs forged in the experience of slavery. Tubman was born in 1820 or 1821 in Maryland and opposed the institution of slavery seemingly from birth. She escaped to freedom through the Underground Railroad when she was twenty-five years old. The woman called "Moses" by her people returned nineteen times to the South and was responsible for leading over three hundred slaves to freedom.[36]

Sojourner Truth was born Isabella Baumfree in upstate New York in 1797. She obtained her freedom in 1827 under New York's gradual emancipation act.[37] In 1843, after a commanding spiritual experience, she adopted the new name Sojourner Truth and became a powerful abolitionist. She had a moving personal presence and used it effectively when speaking. Her speaking was persuasive to many not only because of her sense of presence, but also because of her astute mind, despite the fact that she was illiterate.[38]

These female liberationists shared significant characteristics with Prosser, Vesey, and Turner. They had a fierce hatred of slavery and adopted an activist approach to confronting this evil institution. Their religious faith stirred them to speak and to act on behalf of those who often still bore the external (and internal) shackles of slavery.[39] Many other women were strategic in the struggle for freedom, but without question Harriet Tubman and Sojourner Truth served as influ-

20

ential models for those who believed that there was a direct relationship between faith in God and an activist approach to ridding the country of slavery.[40] Such women have proven effective examples for many liberation-minded African-American women today.

African-American history is an abundant source for black theology. It not only highlights the realities of the development and perpetuation of black culture, but it also includes a narrative of the struggle to affirm that culture. African-American history is a theater where the characters, in various periods and in various life-situations, graphically portray the pain, hope, and determination of African-American people to celebrate their personhood. Foundational in these portrayals is the religious faith of these people and the embodiment of this faith—the black church. Religious faith played a major role in providing a motivation and a plan for these freedom fighters. This activist interpretation of religious faith provides a powerful historical model for black theologians.

Cone suggests that revelation is a second source for black theology. Revelation takes place in concrete historical events occurring in human history. He insists that revelation is incomprehensible within the realm of black theology apart from a consideration of God at work in the black experience.[41] Cone sees Jesus Christ as the pivotal figure in an appropriate interpretation of what God is doing through historical events on behalf of the oppressed because Christ himself is "the complete revelation of God."[42] Just as the resurrection of Christ points to the fact that he is present today, revelation must be understood as a black event that is going on today. Cone argues that black people are involved in liberation now and that God himself is also at work in the process.[43] He holds that God makes an unqualified identification with the liberation of black people in the manifestation of all genuine liberative events. These events are the only means available in this society for an authentic encounter with God.[44]

Third, Scripture is another important source for black theology. Cone holds that the Bible is not the revelation of God; only Christ is. It is, however, an essential witness to God's revelation and is foundational for Christian thinking about God. The Bible serves as an evaluative standard for contemporary interpretations of God's revelation, and the biblical witness is that God unquestionably is a God of liberation.[45] Cone teaches that the Bible is not an infallible witness; God is not the author and the biblical writers are not secretaries. He thus believes that attempts to prove things like verbal inspiration can obscure the real meaning of the text, namely, liberation.[46]

In a more recent book, New Testament scholar Cain Hope Felder voiced a similar concern about the nature of Scripture. He advocates the adoption of a new critical stance toward tradition, toward prevailing exegetical methodologies, and conclusions drawn from questionable hermeneutical analysis. He argues that there is more that requires consideration in black biblical interpretation, and it is in this sphere that his perspective on the nature of the Bible emerges. Felder affirms that the Bible is the "the most important *ancient locus* for the word of God."[47] He maintains that this affirmation does not mean, however, that the Bible is categorically in and of itself the very Word of God.

Fourth, Jesus Christ, to whom the Bible witnesses, is the climactic source for black theology. Cone describes Jesus as the "content of the hopes and dreams of black people."[48] Christ was revered by black slaves because they saw through his liberating presence that he had chosen them. Because he was the Truth he empowered them both to see through the dehumanizing lies of the surrounding white culture and to believe in their own worth. Though black slaves may have been sold like livestock, Jesus was present with them. He was the great burden-bearer and gave them hope to sing,

> Sometimes I hangs my head an' cries,
> But Jesus goin' to wipe my weepin' eyes.[49]

Cone argues that the black experience is a *source* of truth, but it is not the Truth itself. Jesus Christ is the Truth and is the evaluator of all truth claims. There is no truth in Jesus, however, independent of the concrete experience of oppression on the part of dehumanized people in general, and people of color in America specifically.[50] There is a solidarity between the church and the Lord that it confesses. Cone argues that because of this identity, the church can dim the light of its witness if it becomes entangled in heresy. He holds that heresy is "any activity or teaching that contradicts the liberating truth of Jesus Christ."[51] It is a shameful inconsistency for the church to hamper the mission of the Lord, the Liberator.

Finally, the tradition of the church is a source for black theology. Tradition is the compilation of theological reflection arising from the history of the church, from its beginnings to the present day. Cone suggests that it is virtually impossible for any serious student of Christianity to ignore tradition because the New Testament itself is a product of tradition.[52] Black theology consults church tradition, but from a critical, evaluative position. Roberts asserts that there must be a "moratorium" on the Western domination of theological reflection. Theologians from contexts such as Africa and Asia must be allowed to do their own theology.[53] This certainly applies to black theologians. Though informed by tradition, a critical, evaluative position facilitates the incorporation of that which advances liberation and the rejection of that which hinders the full humanization of the oppressed.[54]

Black theology draws upon a number of sources to spawn a body of *orthopraxis,* confession formulated in the midst of liberative activity. The *black experience,* a term encompassing many elements of the historical black experience, is foundational and determinative for black theology. A major part of the black experience has been and continues to be the black church. Revelation, which Cone regards as emerging from, though still distinct from Scripture, is important because at its core it is a witness to God's liberating activity in black history. Scripture has long enjoyed a central role in the lives of black people.

Cone holds that the Bible and tradition are important sources for black theological reflection. Each is important, but they must be examined for potential contributions to the black theological task with an unashamedly critical eye. The issue of biblical hermeneutics focuses attention again not only on the nature of revelation and Scripture, but also on the issue of the authority and the applicability of biblical teaching to black theological praxis. It is a matter that requires more attention. Roberts and Cone have had prominent roles in setting the parameters for a black theological hermeneutic.

The Hermeneutics of Black Theology

Hermeneutics in black theology is developing. Work in Scripture, uncovering its meaning and significance for black theology, continues and reveals a richness of thought unique to individual thinkers in the discipline. Though there are many "texts" that require analysis toward the development and application of black theology, we will focus our attention on the study of Scripture.[55] I will first present what is the dominant theme and organizing principle of black biblical hermeneutics. I will then survey some influential representatives of this methodological perspective. My formal evaluation of this trend in hermeneutics will be developed in the last chapter; thus I am engaged only in description at this point. I will summarize the common characteristics in this discipline from an examination of these representative topics.

James Evans argues that an authentic hermeneutic, or "the act of interpretation,"[56] must advance the primary theme of liberation. Liberation captures "the real, visceral character of the human struggle against the principles of evil in the world."[57] Evans sees liberation as ultimately reflective of God's will and work in creation. Liberation is multidimensional because it includes the physical, spiritual, and cultural aspects of all human existence.[58] Physical liberation refers to an innate desire to have freedom of movement, associations, and self-determination. Spiritual empowerment facilitates a new life characterized by a new hope and a new self-confidence. Cultural liberation entails a freedom from "negative self-images, symbols, and stereotypes."[59]

Evans's hermeneutical philosophy advances his view of the divine plan of liberation by initiating and perpetuating three tasks. The first task is to remind the interpreter(s) that the religious perspective of the world held by white Christians is radically different than that of black Christians. He refers to this as an "epistemological break."[60] It is undoubtedly the goal of a liberative hermeneutic to help African-American Christians to view the world as God views it. That is to say that God sees the world as comprised of, among other things, those in need of liberation. This then is related to the second task of a liberative hermeneutic, namely to deconstruct or take apart the misinterpretations of African-Americans undergirding American Christianity. Evans subsumes the role of hermeneutics under the overarching category of black religion when he writes, "Black religion is a protest against those portrayals of African-Americans as less than human or outside the providential care of God."[61]

A third task for African-American hermeneutics is to promote a true and essential self-knowledge. This is to say that hermeneutics must facilitate affirmation of African-American selfhood. Affirmation comes not only through biblical interpretation but also through an enhanced comprehension of how the situation of oppression emerged in the United States and how it is sustained in the present sociocultural setting.

Evans's multidimensional understanding of liberation provides the consummating theme of the hermeneutics of black theology. Many black theologians exhibit this hermeneutical emphasis, though given this common characteristic, there are, nevertheless, methodological distinctives among them as well. I will survey briefly the unique contributions of Cone, Roberts, and two more recent interpreters, Stephen Reid (an Old Testament and biblical theology scholar) and Cain Hope Felder (a New Testament scholar).

Cone, as I have discussed above, argues that Scripture is foundational for the development of black theology. The meaning of Scripture begins with Israel's belief that Yahweh was involved in their history.[62] Yahweh's relationship with Israel provides the backdrop for the understanding of divine salvation revealed as the liberation of slaves from oppressive social, political, and economic edifices. This salvation (liberation) is the paradigm for what God wills and how God works in the realm of concrete historical situations where people are being dehumanized. This idea of dehumanization is consistent with a comprehensive understanding of oppression. This is to say that when people are made to feel and to believe that they are less than image-bearers of God, having no rights or voice in matters of personal and communal self-determination, they are being dehumanized.

Cone's hermeneutic uses Christology as its point of departure from other hermeneutical systems. Together with the Old Testament tradition of the exodus, Christ's incarnation, death, and resurrection become a further confirmation of God's solidarity with the poor and his work of liberation on their behalf:

> God became a poor Jew in Jesus and thus identified with the helpless in Israel. The cross of Jesus is nothing but God's will to be with and like the poor. The resurrection means that God achieved victory over oppression, so that the poor no longer have to be determined by their poverty.[63]

Christ is the one who models and grants freedom to the oppressed. Hermeneutics essentially becomes that which explicates Christ as the climactic revelation of God's solidarity with the oppressed. Because Christ is God's complete word of liberation, Cone maintains a strong christological focus in his discipline of biblical hermeneutics.[64]

The Bible tells the story of God's deliverance through Jesus Christ. God wills to redeem humanity from the enslaving powers of sin, death, Satan, and the human institutions that are permeated with these realities. Cone, however, insists that the Bible does not contain infallible truths about God or Jesus, but rather has the role of pointing to the power of God—manifested in the life, death, and resurrection of Jesus—that will accomplish liberation. Regarding Philippians 2:6–8, Cone correctly observes that in Paul's presentation, divine glory and power are hidden in the form of a slave. The effect for black people, however, is empowerment:

> Through the reading of Scripture, the people hear other stories about Jesus that enable them to move beyond the privateness of their own story; through faith because of divine grace, they are taken from the present to the past and then thrust back into their contemporary history with divine power to transform the sociopolitical context.[65]

With his handling of this particular passage, Cone maintains the christologically focused empowerment testified to in Scripture.

J. Deotis Roberts also holds that the Bible is essential in the development of a black theological hermeneutic. In a telling juxtaposition of topics, he observes that in a number of ways the African portrayal of God resembles that of God in the Old Testament.[66] This juxtaposition is the product of some basic convictions that Roberts has on the nature of a liberative hermeneutic. I will develop these convictions later in this section. Suffice it here to say that Roberts advocates an "exegesis from below, seen in solidarity with the oppressed, [which] yields insights overlooked by those who read the Bible from the perch of privilege."[67]

Roberts argues that there must be an expansion of the hermeneutical circle "that begins and ends with the Bible reinterpreted."[68] A liberative hermeneutic essential for black theology, as well as for any oppressed people, must move toward three goals. First, a black liberative hermeneutic must be universal in vision. The teaching and norms developed must include the voices and perspectives of "all cultures, and all religions."[69] Second, this hermeneutic must have human rights as its focus. Roberts sees the basis for this concern in the nature of God's work in creation. All human beings have a divine spark in them; thus the issue of human rights is not only for those under the "Christian covenant," but for all humanity.[70] Third, the holistic nature of thought and reality must be fully considered. What is considered by some to be concrete reality is in some form or fashion affected by the realm of the spiritual. He suggests the awareness of the spiritual dimension as the genius of black religion. Black religion, particularly through the example of determinative leadership, demonstrates a remarkable balance between a consistently evident social consciousness and a goal of living in spirituality. According to Roberts, the "secular and sacred, the rational and the mystical, the individual and social interact and are held in dynamic tension in one continuum of experience."[71]

To grasp Roberts's hermeneutic, we must consider the fact that he, like Cone, thinks theologically as he studies the particulars of Scripture. He shows this tendency in the following statement:

> Theologically, Jesus was obsessed with the "righteousness of God." This has to do with the ethical attributes of God. Jesus came preaching that the kingdom of God is at hand (Mark 1:15). The "kingdom" of which he spoke is equivalent to the "will of God." Thus, to "seek the Kingdom" is to seek righteousness (Matt. 6:33).[72]

Roberts sees the righteousness of God in terms of ethical attributes of God, that is, as a consideration of why God acts the way he does when he chooses to act. His treatment of

Scripture becomes not only a presentation of the particulars that are present in the passages, but it also becomes a mandate for people to seek the will of God through doing what is right. There is no detailed exposition of the passages, but rather an incorporation of them to bring together the physical and spiritual elements of a life focused on love of God and love of neighbor.

Cain Hope Felder is a New Testament scholar, but his analyses of specific biblical texts show a similar concern with liberation in ways other than the so-called spiritual way. Through study of the gospels and the apostle Paul, Felder formulates the following as a basic understanding of freedom in the New Testament:

> It is more accurate to take Paul's use of the word *freedom* in a comprehensive or holistic manner, for a "free spirit" inescapably guides the body toward freedom. Thus for Paul, no less than for Jesus himself, the good news was a full rejection of discriminating against persons or deferring to the wealthy or powerful by virtue of their social position or outward appearance (Rom. 2:11).[73]

The largely Gentile churches in the region of Galatia were facing enormous pressure from Jewish Christian missionaries to conform to the law. Felder understands passages like Galatians 3:28 and 5:1 as calls to maintenance of the believers' relationship and status with Christ, a maintenance that may involve various forms of resistance. This is often the price of freedom. Freedom is maintained and experienced further when there is responsible involvement in the community that demonstrates love for one another.[74] Felder's exegetical findings lead him to conclude that the freedom both to preserve personhood against enslaving forces and to show and experience love in community are divine mandates.

Stephen B. Reid, an Old Testament and biblical theology scholar, also holds that black church tradition informs the interpretation of Scripture. Black church tradition and biblical interpretation are not prioritized one over the other:

> Neither identity nor interpretation takes priority; they act as partners. The black biblical scholar, theologian, and preacher hold black culture and tradition in the one hand and the Bible in the other.[75]

Accordingly, a black hermeneutic has a twofold task. It must first engage the text in a serious way. Second, it must show how the biblical texts are adaptable toward the fulfillment of human potential and the establishment of community in the midst of a racially and socioculturally hostile environment.[76]

Reid maintains that the exegetical method for a black biblical tradition has three dynamically related movements. It begins with a critical reading of the biblical text. This reading provides the black church with an awareness of the "political, social, and economic realities of antiquity."[77] The second movement involves the recovery of black biblical interpretation. Parallels between the situation of God's people in the Bible and black people's situation in the United States are explored. This exploration leads the black biblical interpreter into application, the third movement, which is a priority that dominates black church tradition.[78] Reid maintains that Christ pervades these movements with a call both to imitation and to victory.[79]

These three movements provide a structure through which the black experience can be analyzed by focusing on three themes Reid holds as integral to the black experience. These themes are unity, patriotism, and suffering/critical awareness. He suggests that unity provides the determinative base for black interpretation of Scripture. The black experience demands that unity be defined as an assimilation in life of cultural and material elements. The cultural dimension is found in the music, art, and theology of black culture.[80] It maintains the unique identity of the black community in the midst of the dominant white community. The realities of black life, namely the effects of racism and capitalism, comprise the material elements. Reid argues that this interplay of the cultural and the material is manifested in the biblical tradition as well, and thus provides a rich source for identifying and applying desirable models for the black community.[81]

Reid's second theme, patriotism, is an arresting term when applied to an interpretation of the black experience. Black patriotism refers to a loyalty to a nation and its ideals, particularly where freedom and justice are held as "inalienable rights."[82] He is convinced that blacks have long been loyal to the American system and that this contributes to the traditional theology of the black church. Theology has been affected in the black church through continued contact with the white church. The primary difficulty, however, which is pervasive in the history of relationships between blacks and whites in the United States, is that blacks consistently have been the recipients of disloyalty in a nation that does not consistently live up to its ideals. Reid holds that patriotism and loyalty are measured ultimately in relationship to the God of freedom. God is the focal point of patriotism and loyalty. No nation or government has the right to demand such expressions that are reserved for God alone. This, Reid argues, is one of the lessons derived from the exodus tradition.[83] God alone is worthy of the total commitment of the people.

Finally, suffering/critical awareness is an essential theme in the black experience as reflected through the use of a black hermeneutical methodology. The past experience of slavery and the present experience of suffering demand explanation. When Scripture is consulted and interpreted, Reid argues that a critical awareness of the historical and contemporary use of the Bible by oppressors must be functioning in the method of the black biblical interpreter. He observes that this critical awareness is what scholars call a "hermeneutic of suspicion."[84] This perspective extends to a needed determination by black biblical teachers and preachers of what constitutes the biblical canon.[85]

Further, through the use of higher critical methodologies, the interpreter can unmask power relationships and institutions in the text while simultaneously seeing streams of liberative tradition that sometimes lay hidden beneath the surface of the various biblical records. These liberative streams are in need of appropriate treatment to yield their transforming potential. For example, Reid claims,

> The critical reading of any biblical text must begin with an examination of the socio-political context of the passage. The material in Genesis 2–4 was brought together by the Yahwist, a tenth-century collection of editors sponsored by kings David and Solomon. The goal of this material was to validate the social order of tenth century B.C.E. Israel. In order to accomplish this task, the stories describe tenth-century practices and label them as the will of God from the beginning.[86]

My purpose here is not to criticize the use of higher critical methodologies in the study of Scripture. It is to point out the sensitivity demonstrated to status-maintaining power relationships behind the text itself. This is something that a growing number of black theologians consider in the reading of the Bible. This does not preclude the Bible as a liberative source; it must be read, however, with the experiences and needs of the black community as a lens.

Reid concludes that the resultant teachings and models then provide three types of black biblical theology. The theme of unity provides a means to survey issues arising from pastoral theology. The theme of patriotism/loyalty lends itself to analyze the liturgical tradition of the black church. Finally, the theme of suffering/critical awareness gives rise to an exploration and implementation of a political theology.[87]

In light of the significance of hermeneutics in black theology, I will outline some general characteristics of a black biblical hermeneutic according to the thought of Cone, Roberts, Felder, and Reid. It is not my purpose here to repeat and assess the distinctives of each interpreter's system. We have observed for example that Cone has a pronounced christological focus in his hermeneutic. Roberts sees the centrality of Jesus Christ in the Christian faith in general and hermeneutics in particular, but also insists on a broader base of input for a black liberation hermeneutic necessary to facilitate liberation for all regardless of sociocultural distinctives. Felder sees biblical interpretation as validated through its contribution to human freedom. Reid attributes much in hermeneutical methodology to the totality of the black experience and then contributes further by offering readings from the biblical texts to address the black situation of oppression. Distinct contributions exist, but I will now focus on some common characteristics of black liberation hermeneutics in light of the discussion above.

First, the experience of racial oppression as it relates to the specific discipline of biblical interpretation leads inescapably to a hermeneutical suspicion (Reid's "critical awareness"). This means that within a framework of determining appropriate biblical teaching and models to provide solutions to the condition of black oppression, black biblical interpreters must be conscious of the ways biblical interpretation in the dominant culture has contributed to oppression. This legitimates the need for a new interpretive model for the black biblical scholar in the midst of the dominant biblical scholarly realm. As we have already seen, the experience of oppression affects the selection of suitable teaching passages, biblical models, and even the limits of the biblical canon.

Second, holistic liberation is the goal of hermeneutics. Liberation encompasses not only the experience of blacks but oppressed people everywhere. Oppression can take many forms, from class to gender, affecting people in many lands and in many ethnic groups. All aspects of existence must be removed from that which inhibits the expression of the full humanity and potentiality of the marginalized in society.

Third, in the analysis of oppression, sociocultural factors occupy a position of prominence. The study of Scripture itself is determinative as a source for black liberative theology, but experiential matters affect interpretation of Scripture. Scripture is a source, but how and to what extent it is used varies with the individual thinkers. Sociocultural factors dominate and involve not only matters of race, but also politics and economics. Together these factors constitute a type of "text" that must be analyzed and interpreted in order to identify long-term remedies.

The Task of the Black Theologian

Rebecca S. Chopp and Mark Lewis Taylor write that theology in the United States

> has undergone a shift from using a melting pot model, in which theology as officially understood sought a dominant or common human experience, to a model that values the collage of different faces, voices, styles, questions, and constructs. Black theologies, Asian-American theologies, feminist theologies, womanist theologies, theologies from gay men and lesbian women, and theologies offered from the perspectives of the disabled are all presented on the scene today.[88]

This is undoubtedly a credible witness to the contemporary world of theological reflection. Black theology is a part of this world, and thus it can inform and be informed by those from diverse theological perspectives. For the black theologian, however, the dehumanization, pain, hopes, and aspirations of the black community are his or her consummating focus.

Cone succinctly states the task of the black theologian: "The task of the theologian, as a member of the people of God, is to clarify what the Church believes and does in relation to its participation in God's liberating work in the world."[89] The church is a community that confesses God's liberating presence is uniquely found in Jesus Christ and commits itself to participate in fulfilling God's will. To fulfill this task the theologian functions in the roles of exegete, prophet, teacher and preacher, and philosopher.

Cone argues that the black theologian is first and foremost an exegete of both Scripture and life. Exegesis involves the study of Scripture as a primary source for theological reflection, but it is also God's Word to those whose lives are suppressed by dehumanizing forces through varied forms of oppression. The black theologian interprets Scripture in light of the survival needs of the oppressed.[90]

Second, because the black theologian is an exegete, he or she is also a prophet. Cone holds that the prophet's message must be one that brings the gospel into confrontation with the injustice of modern society. The pervasiveness of injustice is itself an effect of past dehumanization and oppression in American history. Because of God's power and the fact that he will bring judgment, there is reason for the hope that justice will indeed reign. This hope is the foundational motivation for advocating and activating liberation processes in the present.

Third, the black theologian is a teacher. The Christian faith must be taught and this teaching must clarify the relationship between faith and human existence. The depths of Scripture and church tradition are plumbed to show how the struggles of the apostles and the church fathers (and mothers) relate to the present-day struggles of the oppressed. The teacher is a communicator, and it is in the context of communication that the teacher is also a preacher. The preacher must proclaim God's word of liberation. Cone correctly argues that here the theologian demonstrates awareness of the "*passionate* character of theological language," which is "the language of celebration and joy that the freedom promised is already present in the community's struggle for liberation."[91]

Fourth and finally, the black theologian is a philosopher, one who is adept at identifying other viable interpretations of life. The truth of the gospel must be demonstrated continually against the backdrop of real human existence. For many, this existence involves oppression. The presentation of the gospel must provide answers in ways that address the form and content of the questions of the oppressed. Cone suggests that it is the philosophical side of the theological task that facilitates intellectual honesty and consistency in the thought and discourse of the theologian. Philosophy enhances openness to other views and protects against inordinate dogmatism.

The task of the black theologian is to clearly explain to the people of God how the gospel of Jesus Christ corresponds to the struggle for liberation. The theologian functions as an exegete, a prophet, a teacher and preacher, and a philosopher within the situation of active involvement. By active involvement, Cone and others mean that the black liberation theologian is not just a speaker or writer, but one who is actively involved in the lives of oppressed people. Cone argues that any theologian who does not center his or her theology on the question of what the gospel has to do with the struggle for liberation by the oppressed has ignored what he sees as the essence of the gospel.[92]

Black theologians raise some serious questions for the church, particularly in the context of the United States, where there has been a peculiar relationship existing historically between the white and African-American races. This peculiar relationship has affected the church, and the church has affected this relationship both positively and negatively. We live today, however. Therefore we now turn our attention to an exploration of what black theology has to say to the evangelical church in the United States.

2
What Can Black Theology Teach the Evangelical Church?

Theological formulation and application are more than a consultation with components such as biblical studies, doctrinal history, philosophy, and denominational tradition. They are affected by the questions and issues posed from inquirers within the church and from those outside the church as it ministers in the contemporary context.

The church not only ministers in the present, but through its encounter with the contemporary milieu it also receives a ministry. It receives that ministry when it is confronted with reminders of certain essential bounds of existence, namely, what the church is and what the church should be doing. In any era some in the church may presume to be well within these bounds reflectively and functionally. The emergence of theological and ethical systems of thought that are not considered mainstream—including black theology—can effectively challenge such presuppositions.

Many within the church assume too quickly that they know what the church is and that it is doing all it should do. Black theology confronts much of what may be considered North American Christianity, but the discipline has distinct concerns and expressions as well. It is, nevertheless, both a product of and a confronter of North American Christianity often spoken of as "church." Some reflections on my meaning of church are essential for a development of this thesis. When I speak of church I am speaking of a body of people identified with certain characteristics.

I will discuss the nature of the church in the next section. In subsequent sections I will explore the contextual nature of theology, the church's adoption of a prophetic stance, and the need for dialogue with the theology of the two-thirds world. These topics were selected because I hold them to be determinative areas where the church has need of confrontation or reminder.

The Definition of Church

The legitimate question may be raised at this point, "What right do you have to define what the church is?" My response is threefold. First, traditions arising from reflections on biblical communities of believers inform our meaning of church. The early church fathers, the medieval period, and the Reformation each provide various trajectories of church development that can help us understand the nature of the church. Second, I come from a particular church tradition that shares many beliefs with the church movement of which I am presently a part.[1] It is this church movement that I seek to address regarding the issue of what it can learn from black theology. Third, I concede the right of anyone or any group to modify the definition of church to suit their purposes. I maintain the right, however, to disagree with their definitions and purposes.

There is much in terms of biblical and historical views on the nature of the church that affirm some authoritative and time-tested characteristics. My attempt at a firm definition will inculcate some observations from the perceptive study of the church by Avery Dulles.[2] His study analyzes five models of the church and how each model responds to three questions.

Dulles argues that these models "serve to synthesize what we already know or at least are inclined to believe. A model is accepted if it accounts for a large number of biblical and traditional data and accords with what history and experience tell us about the Christian life."[3] These models are (1) the church as institution; (2) the church as mystical communion; (3) the church as sacrament; (4) the church as herald; and (5) the church as servant. This section is not intended as a fully-developed theology of the church. There are, for example, many metaphors of the church in Scripture alone. My purpose here is to arrive at a foundational definition. Definition is essential because it speaks to the nature and mission of the church, particularly as it relates to issues of race and ethnicity.

The church as an institution brings together certain features that should not be thought of as totally exclusive to this model, but rather as those that together give it a certain degree of uniqueness. That is to say that other models may include some of these features. The institutional model, however, brings together a combination of characteristics with varying degrees of intensity in manifestation. Dulles, drawing primarily from his Roman Catholic background, holds that there are three powers and functions of the institutionalized church: teaching, sanctifying, and governing.[4] These functions are carried out through a "hierarchal conception of authority."[5] Any attempts at racial and ethnic unity, then, would be largely a function of the vision of leadership.

The model of the church as a mystical communion draws together some important characteristics of both a sociological and metaphysical nature. In this model the church shares commonalities with what Charles H. Cooley describes as "primary groups": "(1) face-to-face association; (2) the unspecialized character of that association; (3) relative permanence; (4) the small number of persons involved; (5) the relative intimacy among the participants."[6]

What solidifies the uniqueness of the church is the metaphysical dimension, the individual and corporate union with

Christ through his Spirit. Dulles sees a harmony between the church as mystical communion and two prominent biblical images: the body of Christ and the people of God. The body of Christ summates the realities of organic unity with Christ through the Spirit and the mutualities of union, concern, and dependence among the members of the body of Christ.[7] The church as the people of God draws rich imagery from the Old Testament. Israel as the people of God was the object of God's special preference, and the same could certainly be said of the church as the people of God.[8] This relationship would in turn call for a responsibility for manifesting this mystical union with Christ and the other members of the body both in the church itself and in daily life. Meditation upon and implementation of the reality of mystical union with Christ could undoubtedly provide a strong foundation for racial and ethnic reconciliation.

The church as sacrament calls attention to what some understand as a fuller and more specific manifestation of God's gracious relationship with creation, particularly man and woman. Dulles observes that a Christian biblical faith holds that God, who is rich in mercy, wills to commune with men and women despite their sinfulness and resistance to grace. Jesus Christ is "the sacrament of God" toward men and women, a divulgence of God's acceptance and rejuvenation despite their unworthiness.[9] The church is a sacrament because it is a visible sign of the redeeming grace of Christ while it facilitates an actualization of this grace in the lives of men and women. The church as sacrament has both an outer and inner aspect. The institutional or structural aspect of the church is required for the visibility of the community of faith in the world. This visibility is more than just the observed physical structures occupied by a group taking part in rituals. The demonstration of unity between churches, Dulles argues, is required for a credible witness to the church's communion with the Lord.[10] This leads to the inner aspect of the church—the presence of real faith, hope, and love among real men and women. The grace of God is evident when this actualizing grace is undeniably demonstrated in the life of the community, both individually and corporately. Racial and ethnic reconciliation would be a sign of believers' unity in Christ and would then be a growing force to bring about harmonious relationships in the world.

The difference between the church as sacrament and the church as herald is the primacy of word over sacrament. The church is a function of the proclamation and acceptance of the gospel. The church's primary mission then is to preach the word that "it has heard, believed, and been commissioned to proclaim."[11] Dulles also observes that this same word not only constitutes the church, but also continually calls the church to repentance and reform.[12] The foundational bond of communion in this model is faith viewed as a response to the proclamation of the Christ-event and its salvific significance. The church, in turn, must proclaim the gospel of Jesus Christ regardless of its racial or ethnic constituency.

A highly attractive model that inspires much reflection in the realm of contemporary understandings of the church's mission is the church as servant.[13] Dulles maintains that since the beginning of modern times, the world has become increasingly independent of the magisterial influence of the church. In the Roman Catholic tradition, Vatican II marked a significant change in the church's self-understanding and missionary strategy in the world. Foundational to this change is the conviction that the church should consider itself as a part of the larger human community and share the same concerns as those outside the church.[14] Christ came not to be served but to serve (Mark 10:45),[15] thus providing a model for the church to follow in the world.

The church as servant calls for more attention in service before God to be directed outside of the formal, structural bounds of the church. Dulles correctly observes that in recent Latin American theology there has emerged an all-encompassing conviction that church leadership in particular and the church in general should identify with the oppressed in their struggle for social, economic, and political liberation.[16] As we observed in chapter one, black theologians would agree on this as the mission of the church, though the mission as conceived in black theology shows derivation more from theological and christological reflections than from ecclesiological reflections.

Dulles ask three questions of each model: (1) How does the model envision the bonds that unify the church? (2) Who are the beneficiaries of the church's ministry? and (3) What is the nature of the benefits that the church bestows on its community?[17] He also contributes a concise assessment of each model's strengths and weaknesses.[18]

Though Dulles's work unquestionably advances ecclesiological reflection on a broader scale, his analysis does not specify the characteristics of the church tradition that I seek to address. His Roman Catholic background and lack of inclusion of ecclesiological discussions from evangelical Protestant scholars[19] make it difficult for Dulles to specify what I believe are the central features of my own evangelical church tradition. Much of my Baptist heritage could be subsumed, for example, under the categories from Dulles's analysis on the models of the church. The nature of these features to which I refer facilitates, on the one hand, the specificity that I see as essential toward an identity of my tradition, while on the other hand, it allows for a discussion of characteristics that transcend denominational differences as well. I will identify these features by consulting a helpful work by Alister McGrath.[20]

McGrath suggests a number of elements he feels are essential to evangelicalism. The first is the consummate authority of Scripture as a source for the knowledge of God and as a mentor for the Christian life.[21] The authority of Scripture rests on God's revealing activity in the biblical material itself as well as in the continuing processes of both interpreting Scripture and applying its teaching internally and externally to the lives of believers.[22] Scripture contains both objective truth and subjective relevance on all matters that it addresses. It speaks to the real needs of people in a way that summons a sense of its authority.[23] Scripture is espoused further as a safeguard against the total enculturation of Christianity. This faith is expressed in dogmatic confessions as well as in socio-cultural garb. The Christian church must maintain a major tension, however, between manifesting realistic and relevant life. It must follow cultural norms in a particular time-space setting. At the same time the church must maintain a transcendent perspective whereby these same cultural norms do not overpower its standards of truth, ethics, and morality.[24]

The inability or unwillingness of the church to maintain this tension has led, at various times and in various ways, to the enslavement of the church to harmful ideologies. For our purposes the issue of racism is dominant. The church's historically inadequate purging of this disease from its midst was expressed in numerous ways, including the marginalization of African-Americans in theological training and dialogue, which has contributed negatively to the rise of black theology. This marginalization can be seen in a lack of intentionality on the part of many evangelical colleges and seminaries, which is shown in at least four ways.

First, there is a lack of intentionality on the part of many evangelical colleges and seminaries to recruit African-American students. Progress has been made but there is still much ground to make up. Second, a lack of intentionality is manifested when administration and faculty at a given institution do not listen to these students to learn firsthand what it means to be an African-American in the United States. Third, there is a lack of intentionality in encouraging larger numbers of African-American students to pursue advanced degrees. This encouragement must take the form of both verbal and financial support. I cannot overemphasize the need for verbal reinforcement. Without affirming voices we cannot achieve our goals. Consistent, non-patronizing encouragement would be a powerful ministry. Fourth, we can demonstrate greater intentionality in hiring African-American biblical and theological scholars. We can learn from them just as we learn from scholars in other disciplines.

A second characteristic of evangelicalism is the central importance of Jesus Christ. Scripture, as the authoritative witness, focuses on him as resurrected (John 20:15–20; Rom. 1:4), as the One who is fully God (Phil. 2:6) and fully man (Matt. 1:1–17; Luke 3:23–37; Rom. 1:3) and as the mediator between God and humanity (1 Tim. 2:5), thus facilitating reconciliation (Rom. 5:9–11). McGrath observes that this christological focus has a number of significant implications for evangelicalism. First, this focus has consistently maintained that it is impossible to stand in faithfulness to the New Testament witness to Jesus Christ without considering Jesus in transcendent categories. He is more than a historical figure. He is more than some great moral teacher.[25] He is God incarnate.

The second implication of evangelicalism's christological focus is that this commitment to the deity of Christ undergirds numerous biblical and theological confessions.[26] Our salvation depends upon the identity of Jesus as the Christ, the Son of God. Third, the cross occupies a central place in evangelical thought as both the ultimate commentary on the woeful condition of humanity apart from the grace of God and as proof of the offer of reconciliation. A fourth implication of the centrality of Jesus Christ is reflected in the doctrine of justification.[27] We are saved "on account of Christ, through faith." This affirms that because of who Jesus is and what he accomplished on the cross, all that was needed to purchase the redemption of those who respond to Him in faith has been done. Fifth, this christological focus spurs believers into evangelism. McGrath encapsulates the relationship between the person and work of Christ and the call to evangelism when he writes,

> To recognize Jesus Christ as our Savior and Lord is to proclaim him as the Savior and Lord of others. Evangelism is no

optional extra, no add-on to the basic gospel package. It is an integral element of the evangelical recognition of the identity and significance of Jesus Christ.[28]

Though it may be regarded by some as an undesirable and archaic endeavor to proclaim such an exclusive, evaluative message as the singularity of Christ as Savior and salvation in him alone, that is what evangelicals claim as the message of Scripture.

The third essential feature of evangelicalism is an emphasis on the lordship of the Holy Spirit. It is the Spirit who facilitates the needed capacities for rebirth (1 Cor. 2:14; 2 Cor. 3:17–18), affirms the internal witness of belonging to God (Rom. 8:15–17), and performs the work of conforming believers to the image of Christ (Rom. 8:29).[29] Full credence is given to the experiential work of the Spirit in the life of the believer as well as in the believing community. This work, however, is in conjunction with and evaluated by the Scriptures.[30]

Fourth, evangelicalism stresses the need for personal conversion. McGrath correctly states that Christianity "is a living and dynamic personal relationship with the crucified and risen Christ."[31] Unfortunately, a person could indulge in an impressive discourse on the nature of salvation without the participant coming to the realization of personal sin, personal accountability before God, and desperate need of personal salvation through faith in Jesus Christ. Wayne Grudem captures the meaning of conversion when he writes, "Conversion is our willing response to the gospel call, in which we sincerely repent of sins and place our trust in Christ for salvation."[32] This is a desired response to the gospel message communicated through the Word and the life of the redeemed community.

The significance of the spoken word leads us to evangelism, the fifth essential feature of evangelicalism. Though regarded by some as obscurantist and unsophisticated, evangelism exhibits faithfulness to the Lord and to his call as set forth in Scripture.[33] The church is called to preach the gospel that confronts men and women with their sin and their alienation from God, while offering forgiveness and reconciliation through faith in Jesus Christ.

The sixth essential characteristic of evangelicalism is an appreciation for Christian community. The church must be faithful to the ministry of evangelism, but it must also be a sphere of influence, a community that nurtures, teaches, and sends new believers. This communal perspective of the church is a desperately needed reminder to believers in this present age of individualism. McGrath sees a correspondence between the evangelical view of community and the tasks of Christian theology:

> Evangelicalism rejoices in the Pauline image of the church as the body of Christ, realizing that this points to a corporate rather than individualistic conception of the Christian life. The "community of Christ" is integral to an evangelical understanding of the Christian life and is of growing importance to evangelical understandings of the tasks of Christian theology.[34]

It is these elements characterizing the evangelical church that I seek to address. Black theology may contribute to the ways in which the church reflects upon and manifests these characteristics, sometimes inconsistently, through the channels of the sociocultural surroundings of the United States. The three areas I will discuss in the remainder of this chapter are, first, the reminder of the contextual nature of theology. This will seek to undermine any type of theological "imperialism" among some. This imperialism could be represented by the statement, "Our way of speaking of God and his relationship to all creation is the only true and pure way to speak of these matters." Second, I will address the need for the church to adopt a more prophetic stance on the specific matters of racism and the potential tolerance of systemic sin. Finally, I will comment briefly on the matter of the church's need to listen more intently to the church of the two-thirds world in the areas of theological formulation and practice.

I realize that in the course of my analysis I may be doing a tremendous injustice to many individual members of the church of Jesus Christ. There are many who are models of Christlike love and commitment to all with whom they come into contact. The church, however, is not totally unlike its societal surroundings. We are still in days of racial tension and division, and it is sheer naivete to believe that a follower of Jesus Christ living and ministering in this present setting is automatically and completely immune to such influences.

The Contextual Nature of Theology

Robert Schreiter suggests that there is much contemporary theological reflection about the content of a theological system, as well as the sociocultural setting from which this system arose. He argues that

> [w]ithout such an initial analysis, a theology readily can become either irrelevant or a subtle tool of ideological manipulation. There is now a realization that all theologies have contexts, interests, relationships of power, special concerns—and to pretend that this is not the case is to be blind.[35]

'All theology is in some sense a "local theology," that is, a system of thought that emerges from the interplay of the gospel, the church, and culture. Schreiter sees each of these elements as multifaceted,[36] but basically the gospel is the proclamation of the Lord Jesus Christ as Savior, and the church is the very presence of the Lord in a given community. The church has a double-lensed perspective: one eye is on the foundational traditions of the faith, while the other eye is on the community and its culture, which comprises all the factors that make up the way of life for the people.

At this juncture some may be concerned that I am mounting an attack upon the historical orthodox faith passed on from the Scriptures. Am I attempting to argue that all theological reflection, in light of our pervasive postmodern direction,[37] is relative in the sense that such reflection is merely the product of and only authoritative for any and all "local" communities? Let me try to allay some of these fears, because they run the danger of preventing some from grasping my main concerns.

I am presently a member of a theologically conservative seminary community, and at the beginning of each school year we collectively stand before God in the sight of each other and affirm our doctrinal statement. This is not a meaningless ritual to me. As I read each statement ranging from confession of a belief in the Triune God to the fact that the Lord Jesus Christ is personally and bodily coming again, I see not only the statements, but also the people who formulated and defended these doctrines, sometimes at great personal cost, throughout the history of the church. I encounter afresh the biblical foundations for such teaching, and I am awed and humbled. There is also a profound and enhanced sense of community at these times. Through the Lord's empowerment I am a defender of the faith (Jude 3). I am aware, however, that specific discussions on theological issues and the exploration of appropriate applications, given particular settings, are not always pursued at the same time or in the same way. Sometimes these differences are not determinative, but considering the history of the United States, the lack of pursuit of application in race relations is very significant. Black theologians voice insensitivities, inconsistencies, and blatant hypocrisy on the part of the dominant white church traditions.

David Cunningham has argued that theology is "a form of persuasive argument."[38] The church has a foundational model of persuasion in the apostle Paul: "Since, then, we know what it is to fear the Lord, we try to persuade men" (2 Cor. 5:11a). That which advances conversion to the Lord Jesus Christ and the disciplines of discipleship is the work of the Holy Spirit through the evangelists (Titus 1:3; 3:5–6), but Paul's example also alerts us to the need for a strategy of persuasion. It is for the sake of effective persuasion among critics that I raise this issue of the contextual nature of theology.

Paul also wrote in the second part of 2 Corinthians 5:11, "What we are is plain to God, and I hope it is also plain to your conscience." Crucial to effective persuasion is the life of the communicator. Herein is the problem for members of the evangelical church according to the black theological community. Our lives call our theological formulations and applications, or lack of applications, into question. The contextual nature of theology requires a periodic reexamination of the content and practice of our theology whereby we can remedy any lack of clarity in thought and consistency of action. This reminder about the contextual nature of theology will also further illuminate two other related issues. First, how and why did black theology begin and then develop as a theological system? Second, why is it that many supporters of black theology will not readily consider what members of the evangelical community have to say?

Theological systemization itself may communicate messages beyond the specifics of content. For example, during my days as a seminary student I was introduced to the discipline of ethics. I learned that ethics was the study of the standards for moral judgments and conduct for a community. My discomfort with this study was not due to the complexity of the discipline nor the claims by some that all ethical standards were relative because of the influence of unique communal questions and issues.[39] I was troubled at the beginning because ethics was a separate course among the core requirements for biblical and systematic theology majors. My naive assumption was that principles of morals and behavior would be drawn directly from reflections on revelation, providence, sanctification, and the like in the core classes themselves. Another problem was that a person or community could engage in the study of ethics without being personally confronted and challenged to live a life "worthy of the calling you have received" (Eph. 4:1).

The black church's experience of slavery and racism in this country did not allow it to discuss and formulate a "docetic" theology, that is, a theology that is so spiritually and theoretically detached that it cannot address specific burdens and issues in a given sociocultural setting. Separations such as biblical and systematic study apart from immediate ethical application are not characteristic of the black church.[40] Tony Evans, for example, addresses the nature of christological reflection performed by slaves:

> The slaves saw Jesus as a present reality, providing the impetus, support, and direction for their journey. The experience of slavery never allowed the black church to get caught up in the theological and philosophical meaning of Jesus, because the Jesus in black religion was a practical deliverer of the oppressed. Neither, however, did they allow this temporal emphasis to decrease their appreciation of the deity of Christ.[41]

This immediate connection between the theoretical and the practical, comparable to much of the process of thought in black theology,[42] has been repeatedly shown in the black church. The reflective nature of white theology can contribute much to the black church particularly in the realm of constructing the means to test for and maintain the standards of orthodoxy. Biblical studies and historical theology place one in a deeper awareness of the sources and construction of confession. Logic can be used to test both the consistency of meaning attributed to words and the internal consistency of arguments. Black theology unquestionably contributes to these areas as well, but continually challenges white theology to be consistent in applying theology to life.

The dominant white church community, however, needs to be reminded of the contextual nature of theology so that it may understand that the issues of concern to the black church are commensurate with the views of members of the black theology community. Many in the black church may not be as concerned about the particulars of tribulational and millennial debates, while they would discuss at length the nature of the kingdom of God and its significance in this temporal setting.[43] Some, however, may have critical concern with the theology and ministry of people like Cotton Mather (1663–1728) and Jonathan Edwards (1703–58) because they owned slaves.[44] Charles Hodge (1797–1878), considered by many in the evangelical community as a respected and influential theologian, wrote a piece defending the institution of slavery.[45] My intent in mentioning these people is not to malign them or to deny their contributions to the church of Jesus Christ. It is simply to suggest two things. First, we have examples of a belief system in the church where racism can not only exist, but also gain legitimacy. Second, these examples will also aid members of the white theological community in understanding why many in the black church community do not fully embrace their theology. This theology is the product of the attitudes as well as the systemization of their theological ancestors. A reminder of the contextual nature of theology summons the motivation to listen more intently and to remedy areas of neglect or misapplication.

The Prophetic Stance

In 1 Timothy 3:15, Paul expresses great concern about the conduct of believers in the "household" of God: "If I am delayed, you will know how people ought to conduct themselves in God's household, which is the church of the living God, the pillar and foundation of the truth." Critical for my purposes in this section is the clause that describes God's household. The household is where members exercise a responsibility to each other and ultimately to God for appropriate behavior.[46] Not only is it "the church of the living God," but it is concurrently "the pillar and foundation of the truth." This is to say that the church of the living God supports the truth. This burden entrusted to the church recognizes that the church is a family. The behavior required in the household of God must be affected by what the church is. Anthony Thiselton correctly points out that the meaning of truth in the Pastoral Epistles resides in "the revealed truth of the gospel message." Having said this, however, he further observes that this truth brings blessing to every aspect of the believer's life.[47] Roger Nicole offers a broader, theological significance to truth within the framework of the New Testament. Truth, he says, is "conformity to reality and opposition to lies or errors."[48]

Paul identifies the church not only in terms of a family forged by the truth of the gospel, but also as a community of those who must function as he does in his prophetic role as a defender of truth. This truth both encompasses the gospel message and addresses a view of reality that opposes falsehoods. Paul was one who, like the Old Testament prophets, interpreted sacred history and tradition from the divine perspective.[49] The church was called to do the same through its community life, proclamation, and teaching. When the church fails in this prophetic role, as in the situations of confronting racism and recognizing systemic sin, it loses credibility and power before the watching world and runs the danger of disapproval before the Lord. The truth claims of the gospel can fairly be questioned by those who see the church's unwillingness to stand for the truth.

Confronting Racism

I am sure there are many in the church who believe that the problem of racism has been effectively eliminated from the body of Christ. Further, they may believe that the church should leave the issue behind and keep "moving forward." They suggest that we need to confront issues such as abortion, the breakdown of the family, and the decay of morals and values in our society. I wholeheartedly agree with such concerns, but we must not be lulled to sleep over the issue of racism and its effects on the church of Jesus Christ. Earlier I said that the church is not totally unlike its surrounding culture. Because the issue of racism still exists in our society,[50] it still exists in the church.

A prominent doctrine of the evangelical tradition in which I was trained is the doctrine of human depravity. Depravity addresses the issue of sin's effects on men and women. Millard Erickson prefers the term *total depravity* and believes it has two primary characteristics.[51] First, sin affects the entire person. It is not encompassed in, nor is it a function of, any one part of the human being. It is pervasive. Even in one's most altruistic efforts, for example, there is a remnant of improper motivation. Second, the sinner cannot separate himself or herself from this condition of contamination. Personal reformation and acceptance before God cannot be accomplished merely through the determination of the individual.

This type of theological reflection is the product of a number of factors, but most germane to these factors is Scripture.[52] My purpose here is not to offer extensive explanation of all passages that contribute to the doctrine of depravity, so I will comment on only a few. Many in the evangelical community would agree that Jeremiah 17:9 ("The heart is deceitful above all things and beyond cure. Who can understand it?") addresses the matter of sin's pervasiveness in a person's life.[53] A passage from the New Testament that has long been understood as describing some infiltrating aspect of sin is Romans 5:12. Though specific points on the nature of our relationship with Adam and the effects of this relationship are debated, it is clear that our membership in the human race places us in position to transgress God's laws, with far-reaching consequences. Douglas Moo sees our solidarity with Adam as the explanation for our mistreatment of each other:

The folly, degradation, and hatred that are the chief characteristics of human history demand an explanation. Why do people so consistently turn from good to evil of all kinds? Paul affirms in this passage that human solidarity in the sin of Adam is the explanation. Whether we explain this solidarity in terms of sinning in and with Adam or in terms of a corrupt nature inherited from him does not matter at this point.[54]

Erickson makes an immediate theological connection between Adam's sin and our sin when, on the basis of Romans 5:12–19 and other Pauline material, he argues that our physical and spiritual constitution comes from our original parents. This means that we inherit, among other things, a corrupted nature.[55]

My purpose here is not to discuss all the relevant details of original sin. It is to focus on some implications of human corruption. Many in the evangelical community would have no problem in accepting the doctrine and would run through a mental list of possible manifestations of this corruption. We would be very conscious of the possibility of impure thoughts, occasional outbursts of anger, and so forth. We may even war against smoking, drinking, and materialism when they are evident among believers. We are shocked when we behold moral and value decay in our society, and we are troubled by things such as abortion and the potential for widespread acceptance of euthanasia. These things are indeed manifestations of our collective, corrupted human nature.

Racism, so some may think, is countered by laws against discrimination in our society. It may still exist, but they believe it is being overcome, and thus is not much of a problem in the church. If Sunday mornings are still the most segregated time of the week, then that is just because of "preference."[56] It seems to me that because of the belief in human depravity, those in the community of faith should be more willing to beseech the Lord to dissect and analyze this "preference" to see whether there are hints of racism there. Some may suggest that we need not deal seriously with this issue in the church because, "I am not responsible for the actions of my ancestors, even if they may have been slave holders, Klansmen, or advocates of segregation in varying degrees of intensity and application."

Those who heard Stephen's speech before the Sanhedrin (Acts 7) may have listened with rapt attention as he began with a short, yet pointed, biblical-historical prologue in response to the charges against him (Acts 6:13–14). Throughout the narrative are interspersed both the works of God, often accomplished through his servants, and the sinful response on the part of many of the people. The relationship between attitude and action, though not prominently stated, can be implied fairly.

Stephen recounts the call of Abraham (Acts 7:2–8), leading to the story of Joseph and the Hebrews in Egypt (7:9–19). Acts 7:9 records the fact that Joseph's brothers were "jealous" of Joseph and sold him into slavery.[57] Stephen then speaks of events in Moses' life (Acts 7:20–38). Though it is not a major point of emphasis within the text itself, I want to make an observation on 7:24 in light of the relationship between attitude and action. Moses is said to have "avenged" his fellow Israelite by striking down the Egyptian. The story then highlights the lack of proper response on the part of the Israelites to Moses as a savior figure (Acts 7:25).[58]

I do not want to lose sight of Luke's concern about the problematic response of the people, but a lesson can be further derived from the background Old Testament text of Acts 7:24, namely, Exodus 2:12. The text states, "Glancing this way and that and seeing no one, [Moses] killed the Egyptian and hid him in the sand." The Lord no doubt used this event to further his plan for Moses and his people. In regard to Moses, however, W. H. Grispen offers a telling comment:

> Moses' act must be condemned, and it was punished by God by his flight to and stay in Midian. But it is striking that a direct punishment by the Lord was not mentioned in so many words. Moses' sin was a quick temper (although his looking

around indicates that there was also some hasty deliberation) and "jumping the gun." He had no right to act as judge. Moses did not yet have a divine appointment; he had not been called. And he lacked the patience to wait for the call.[59]

Moses is an example of a problematic relationship between attitude and action. Without the appropriate attitude of patience the result was the problematic action of murder. Similarly, when there are improper attitudes about race in the church, it will be manifested in some form, in some fashion, through actions.

Stephen addresses other people and events involving evidences of improper motivation and behavior. He brings attention to the rebellious attitude and actions of the Israelites who turned their hearts "back to Egypt" (Acts 7:39) and rejected Moses. They demanded that Aaron build them a god in the form of a calf and they brought sacrifices to "what their hands had made" (v. 41). Joshua and David certainly had many glorious achievements, but they also had their shortcomings (Josh. 9:14–15; 1 Chron. 28:3).

The climactic commentary on this tradition-historical survey comes in Acts 7:51–53. Stephen accuses the Jews of being "stiff-necked," of having "uncircumcised hearts and ears," and of consistently resisting the Holy Spirit (v. 51). Even before he condemns them for similar actions, culminating in the rejection of the Lord Jesus Christ ("the Righteous One," v. 52), he accuses them of being like their fathers. This is not to say that they did every single thing that their fathers did before them, but Steven indicts them for having the same stubbornness, the same impure heart, the same resistance to the work of the Holy Spirit.[60] Actions counter to the will of God result from improper attitudes, though a particular action itself may not be duplicated.

In the predominantly white evangelical church, as I have defined it above, we would readily argue that even believers battle against depravity. They are in need of the continual empowerment of the Holy Spirit to overcome this insidious force. We would agree that in some foundational ways we are "like our fathers." We may lament the decay of moral standards in our society and may even acknowledge that the believing community, unfortunately, is affected negatively by such dynamics. We recognize that "we are not what we should be." At the same time, however, we are often extremely selective about what form this depravity can have in and among us. What many of us are ignorant of—through self-deception at best, or in rebellion at worst—is the possibility of racist attitudes and actions. For some it is difficult to go beyond the matter of the avoidance of members of a particular racial or ethnic group in the name of preference, to an analysis of the nature of this preference. We may find that we are truly "like our fathers," though we may not do the exact same things.

At this juncture I will offer some discussion on the nature of racism and its affects on the church, the community entrusted with the truth. In a penetrating examination and reflection on racism, one I wish I had read much sooner than I did, George D. Kelsey offered this summary of the nature of racism:

> Racism is a faith. It is a form of idolatry. It is an abortive search for meaning. In its early modern beginnings, racism was a justificatory device. It did not emerge as a faith. It arose as an ideological justification for the constellations of political and economic power which were expressed in colonialism and slavery. But gradually the idea of the superior race was heightened and deepened in meaning and value so that it pointed beyond the historical structures of relation, in which it emerged, to human existence itself.[61]

Incorporating arguments from Kelsey, I want to explore the idea of racism as a faith and as idolatry. Fleshing out the implications of racism as contributing to the development of a theology and conceivably an indulgence in idolatry is far beyond the scope of this largely introductory study. I will briefly present three theological areas for this exploration of the effects of racism: God, man/woman, and Christian community.

Before beginning with the first of these areas, I want to address concerns that may exist among some readers. First, I am not presenting the idea that all the problems facing the African-American community in the United States can be attributed to racism. Second, I am not suggesting that racism is the only reason why African-Americans and whites do not always worship together. Third, I am not arguing that racism is the only issue that the church of Jesus Christ needs to confront. It would be very easy to be lulled to sleep, however, thinking racism is no longer a problem in the church because of the progress brought on by the civil rights movement, affirmative action, and the like. My desire is simply that the church aspire to be a credible witness to the gospel, being sure that we are truly defending the faith "entrusted to the saints" (Jude 3) in all possible aspects.

The acts of God tell us much about God.[62] Those who hold Scripture to be the Word of God often hold the view that it is an authoritative interpreter of the acts of God. The accuracy of the authoritative picture of God, leading to the possibility of worshiping and following God, is directly related to the accuracy of the actions attributed to God. Paul expressed great concern about the possibility of presenting a false proclamation of God's acts (1 Cor. 15:15). He and others had given testimony to the fact that God had raised Jesus from the dead. This proclamation (v. 12) would be false if there is no resurrection from the dead. The devastating results of an erroneous message about the resurrection of Christ are clearly delineated (vv. 14–19), but we can also infer that there would be a false picture of how God acts. This in turn could lead to a false picture of who God is. Hearers could be led to seek a god other than the true God.

This concern for an accurate witness of who God is and what he has done is shown in the Old Testament tradition, for example, in the book of Isaiah.[63] Isaiah 43:9–13 reads:

All the nations gather together and the peoples assemble. Which of them foretold this and proclaimed to us the former things? Let them bring in their witnesses to prove they were right, so that others may hear and say, "It is true." "You are my witnesses," declares the LORD, "and my servant whom I have chosen, so that you may know and believe me and understand that I am he. Before me no god was formed, nor will there be one after me. I, even I, am the LORD, and apart from me there is no savior. I have revealed and saved and proclaimed—I, and not some foreign god among you. You are my witnesses," declares the LORD, " that I am God. Yes, and from ancient days I am he. No one can deliver out of my hand. When I act, who can reverse it?"[64]

Israel is called a witness to God. Their true and accurate testimony must incorporate what God has done, things that must not be attributed to someone else. Conversely, though not stated in the text, nothing must be ascribed to God that he did not do. The nations must be confronted when they give false testimony about God. This confrontation would be rendered ineffective if Israel presented a false view of God or essentially another god.

Kelsey argues that racism is a faith system that results in a form of idolatry.[65] It facilitates this idolatry through two potential channels. First, racism often entails a view that a particular race is inherently inferior to another at the fundamental level of being. God has not then created all men and women in his image, that which constitutes humanness, as Scripture teaches (Gen. 1:26–27). The image of God is a foundational point for the establishment of an equality of essential being. Some may believe there are those who are more in his image than others. Given this view, there is attributed to God an action that is not true. Though I disagree with his etiological emphasis for the origin of the narrative in Genesis 2–3,[66] I affirm Steven McKenzie's argument that in this section,

Adam and Eve are described as the parents of all people. This point is explicitly made for Eve, whose name comes from the

Hebrew word for life, so that she is the "mother of all living" (3:20). The story embraces the idea of equality and fraternity among all people, regardless of race. Since all are descended from one couple, all are related, all are a part of one another.[67]

If some ignore the biblical accounts relevant to the issue,[68] then they may suffer the consequences of trusting in a god other than the God of the Bible. There is a danger, then, of not only worshiping another god, which is totally inappropriate for members identified with the redeemed community, but it also invites the Lord's correction (Heb. 12:5–6).

A second channel of racism involves a form of polytheism. Kelsey argues that if a racist is a Christian, which is certainly conceivable in the United States, he or she is frequently a polytheist.[69] Though one may believe that he or she is living under the sphere of God's authority in every way, there is a danger of relinquishing a sphere, or spheres, to another authority regarded as an ultimate. Kelsey cites the work of H. Richard Niebuhr to derive a definition of faith, and its role in a belief system. Faith is a "trust in that which gives value to the self," on the one hand; and on the other, "it is loyalty to what the self values."[70] For the racist, the ultimate (or god) is race. Race occupies a position that rivals the supremacy of God and in turn imparts ultimate value for that person or group.

Kelsey's portrayal of race as a faith system inculcating idolatry may appear to some as extreme, at least initially. His argument, however, seems in line with the prayer of the psalmist, "Search me, O God, and know my heart; test me and know my anxious thoughts. See if there is any offensive way in me, and lead me in the way everlasting" (Ps. 139:23–24). The immediate reasons for this needed internal reflection are the matters of human depravity and our unique history in the United States.

Racism can have an effect in the distinct realm of biblical anthropology, or the study of the nature of humankind.

Though strong dogmatic statements are made in the church that all men and women are created in the image of God, other means of communication may show that many think and behave as if they believe God created two races. Ruth Benedict sees such thinking as a form of naturalism whereby "one group is condemned by Nature to hereditary inferiority and another group is destined to hereditary superiority."[71] There is unquestionably a relationship between one's view of God and his work in creation, and one's view of the human race with its constituencies.

Kelsey disagrees with those who hold that biological distinctions define the essence of some human beings. Rather, he argues that essence is defined by God, who created men and women in his image. Human beings were created so that they may accomplish a number of things,[72] but foundationally that they may exist in relationship with God. There is a crucial distinction among these image-bearers, but it must be understood in the following way:

> In the racist understanding of man, racial variation is a fundamental, structural, human differentiation of polar proportions. To differ in race is to differ in essence. On the contrary, the biblical faith affirms the unity of the human race in creation and destiny. Further, the Bible speaks of only one structural differentiation, and that one is within the human race, namely, male and female.[73]

With a diminished conviction that all men and women are equally made in the image of God comes a danger that members of the "defective" race can do nothing to change the convictions of the "superior" race. Kelsey points out that even elements such as hard work and noble character manifested in members of the so-called inferior race change nothing, because work and nobility can be regarded by the so-called superior race as that which "inheres in his [the inferior race's] unalterably corrupt humanity."[74]

Racism that essentially denies the full presence of the image of God in all men and women regardless of race is a demonic work. It is not that which calls upon Satan for power or independently places members of a particular race under the power of Satan. It simply accomplishes in the heart of the racist something that the demonic realm seeks to achieve in a number of ways, namely, the marring of God's image in a human being. Compare some specific texts in Mark 5:1–20 concerning the appearance and behavior of the Gerasene demoniac. While the man was demon possessed,[75] he was described in the following way:

> This man lived in the tombs, and no one could bind him any more, not even with a chain. For he had often been chained hand and foot, but he tore the chains apart and broke the irons on his feet. No one was strong enough to subdue him. Night and day among the tombs and in the hills he would cry out and cut himself with stones (vv. 3–5).[76]

After Jesus casts out the demons and allows them to enter a herd of pigs that subsequently run down a bank to be drowned in the lake (v. 13), the man is described as "sitting there, dressed and in his right mind" (v. 15). The effect of the demons was to make the demoniac look and act as less than an image-bearer of God. Of course, the event contributed to the establishment of the Lord Jesus' credentials as the King and to the unique breaking-in of the kingdom of God in time and space through his life and ministry. The dehumanizing work of the demons, however, must not be missed.

Some may think at this point that, "I have not done anything like this to anyone. Just because I have a preference to be around my own, how can that even begin to approach any involvement in demonic activity?" The parallel between racism and the work of demons exists in the marring of God's image in human beings. Though the racist may do it only in his or her heart by thinking a certain racial or ethnic group is inferior, or engaging in some harmful stereotypical thought,[77] nevertheless there is a diminishing, a dehumanization of those image bearers. Some may think that the inner attitude ultimately harms no one since it is a private matter. As I will argue later under the issue of systemic sin, that is extremely fallacious thinking.

. Racism adversely affects the manifestations of true Christian community. It is the faith response to the gospel that facilitates our being placed in Christ and thus becoming members of one body (Rom. 3:22–24; 1 Cor. 12:12–13). We do not deny the significance of the individual believer and all that is essential to his or her being.[78] We do not deny the need for a continual, growing personal relationship with Jesus Christ on the part of each believer. The privileges and disciplines of prayer, Bible study, and meditation cannot be neglected. The acid test of the legitimacy of the believer's personal relationship with the Lord, however, is still in the context of community. Undoubtedly, only the Lord knows precisely the state of the believer's position and walk before him, but one could easily misconceive the nature of his or her walk before the Lord. Even Scripture itself does not insure the validity of this walk if the individual believer is the only reader and evaluator. At some time, at some place, this believer must consult with another believer to determine whether there has been true growth in the Lord.

Francis A. Schaeffer argued that John 13:33–35 "reveals the mark that Jesus gives to label a Christian not just in one era or in one locality but at all times and all places until Jesus returns."[79] He further argues that the Lord Jesus has given the watching world the right to evaluate the legitimacy of one's claim to be a Christian on the basis of whether or not this believer bears the mark of the Christian, namely, love.[80] Schaeffer later offers further reflections on the call for the expression of love at the community level, developing the significance of John 17:21: "that all of them may be one, Father, just as you are in me and I am in you. May they also be in us so that the world may believe that you have sent me." If the world does not see true unity among those who claim allegiance to Jesus Christ, Schaeffer suggests, the church should not be surprised when the world is unimpressed with our proclamation that the Father has sent the Son.[81]

For those truly concerned about the credibility of the gospel in a polarized society, the issue of Christian love for one another becomes more crucial. A sincere member of the church may ask legitimately, "How have I not loved my darker-hued brothers and sisters?" I will briefly address this issue and in the process offer a response to those with potentially faulty thinking. I want to speak to my white brothers and sisters who may find it absolutely impossible that they, who have not enslaved anyone, nor lynched anyone, nor personally said anything degrading to or about an African-American, could be a racist. I will simultaneously be addressing African-Americans who think that because they do not have the "power" of the dominant white wing of the church, they cannot be racist.[82]

A fruitful study of expressions of racism hinges on two factors: the power component of this problem and the nature of human beings. Power, from an ideal perspective,

> is the ability or means to accomplish ends. Ideally, power is reciprocal, collaborative energy that engages us personally and communally with God, with one another, and with all of creation in such a way that power becomes synonymous with the vitality of living fully and freely.[83]

A full analysis of this definition is beyond the scope this present work. I will comment briefly on the matter of the "ability or means to accomplish ends." Many will immediately understand the word *power* in terms of larger institutional structures. Racism permeates sociopolitical structures,[84] but its deeper insidious nature is manifested when we think of "ability or means to accomplish ends" at the micro level of human relationships. The reality of racism has much to do with the nature of human beings.

My insight into this realm of racism was further developed in January 1997, when I had the privilege of delivering the Black Awareness Week discourses at Trinity Evangelical Divinity School. I knew that I was speaking to an audience comprised of numerous backgrounds. We may have shared much in terms of a common doctrinal statement, but I was not assured of sharing much more than that with the majority of them. My suspicions were that a significant number of the students and staff could not conceive that a race problem affecting the church truly existed. So, in addition to talking about historical, social, and cultural dynamics, I also made the point that humanization does not occur autonomously. The capacity to experience full humanity is developed in a context of more than one, that is, in community. Affirmation and encouragement are needs of all human beings and are essential to a person's perception that they are loved and esteemed. Even in the church believers can choose to advance or not advance the process of humanization through what they do with the matters of affirmation and encouragement. These things affect what unfolds for a person or group and thus a measure of power is inherently involved in the decision. People can give or deny what is needed by other people on the basis of race.

In this process of humanization even African-Americans have enormous power in affecting the white community, particularly in the church. There are two adverse effects on those who depersonalize others through racist attitudes. First, those who depersonalize others are themselves depersonalized because full humanization occurs in the context of relationship with others. When the members of the other group are relegated to the status of objects, there is no possibility of the truly mutual relationships that are appropriate to a shared humanity. The depersonalized never become persons who are allowed to identify blind spots, insensitivities, and inconsistencies in the subjectors.[85] Thus, the subjectors become dehumanized through their dehumanization of others.

Second, the subjectors do not forge true community. They do not possess a solid, positive foundation for communion. There is diminishing of a transcendent standard whereby their existence and practice can be given true meaning and worth. Their meaning and worth, then, are derived only by the immediate conditions that surround them. The maintenance of power over the subjected race inordinately governs the specifics of life because this is what gives meaning and worth. Such a focus cannot be the bedrock of genuine community. The subjectors cannot see themselves fully, and their lack of vision and understanding of others perpetuates their communal dilemma.[86]

African-Americans, and certainly other minorities in the church, have the power to aid in the humanization of its racist members by not allowing themselves to become objects to them. They must remember and continually apply in day-to-day life the fact that they are also image-bearers of God. An ever-present danger is internalizing what the dominant culture communicates about African-Americans. This internalization can take a number of forms. It can manifest itself in self-rejection whereby despair rules in a person's life, or it can manifest itself in the adoption of a pride that attempts to hide a deep sense of inadequacy. Resentment and mistrust can dominate one's life and are often accompanied by a policy of avoidance of whites under the guise of "I just want to be with my own." Members of the African-American church do not all experience these and other related feelings. My point is that if such dispositions exist among African-Americans and other minorities in the church, they may exercise such influence that participation in the humanization of its racist members is dramatically hindered.

This does not mean that minorities are called to tolerate disrespect in these humanization efforts. It does mean that the African-American member of the church confronts and challenges whenever and wherever it is needed, while continuing to love the problematic members. It is difficult to maintain such a balance. As with the Lord Jesus (Phil. 2:5–11; Heb. 12:2) great patience, sacrifice, and endurance of pain is required.[87] For the integrity of the gospel, though, abandoning any and all attempts to actualize in time and space the reconciliation among believers that the Lord Jesus has facilitated on the cross would be an affront to the grace and glory of God.

On the one hand the most heinous manifestation of racism is to deny, in various forms, the full humanity of other human beings created in the image of God. On the other hand it is equally a crime to withdraw from the process by which others are enabled to become more human. This involvement, or lack thereof, calls for decisions that may be affected by race, and they inherently inculcate a dimension of power over others. It takes a community where there is mutual respect and embracing of all members to humanize one another:

> Through the "Thou" a man becomes "I." Only as "I" allow the other to confront me as "Thou" do "I" stand before him as "I." When he becomes "It" to me, "I" become the correlate of "It." "I become through my relation to the Thou; as I become I, I say Thou."[88]

It takes the totality of the church of Jesus Christ, regardless of race or ethnicity, to bolster the credibility of the gospel in a skeptical, yet searching sociocultural context. We do this by modeling the meaning and significance of the gospel in the context of a loving and affirming, though sometimes a confronting, community.

Systemic Sin

Black theology as a movement reminds the church of the pervasiveness of sin in systems, structures, and sociopolitical institutions. Systemic sin should be thought of as the bentness of human nature manifested in the perpetuation of injustice to, and dehumanization of, select groups in sociocultural constructs.[89] Johannes Baptist Metz, another theologian sensitized to the political implications of theological positions, speaks against a "privatized faith." By this he means a faith that is content to reflect only on one's personal relationship with God without giving additional thought to showing this relationship by demonstrating concern about forces of injustice and dehumanization couched in the societal context in which the believer lives.[90]

For a number of reasons many evangelicals are suspicious of this call for political awareness based on theological convictions. First, there is great concern about undermining orthodox doctrine. The kingdom of God, for example, not only entails the present rule of God (Ps. 103:19) but there is also the reality of the future full establishment of the kingdom (Matt. 25:31, 34). Among those who want to maintain this balance and consider the kingdom as the working out of justice and humanization in the temporal world, there may be a lack of needed reflection on the future, cataclysmic fulfillment of the kingdom. The call for personal repentance for personal sin before God may also be compromised.

Second, some theological positions can foster an otherworldly perspective in matters affecting social and political issues. A premillennialist who believes in a future physical rule of Christ on the earth for a period of one thousand years[91] may hold a rather pessimistic attitude toward human culture and social involvement. The implication for some premillennialists may be that Christ will return to find rampant moral decay, and thus why get involved in delaying the inevitable? This is just one illustration of how one's theological views can affect one's assessment of engagement with society and government.

Erickson offers some helpful commentary on the nature and effects of social sin.[92] Much is essentially an amplification of 1 John 2:16 and Ephesians 6:12. His discussion on "corporate personality" is a critical and timely discussion in light of the tendency in our present society, as well as in the church, to be highly individualistic. The lack of appreciation for the vital relationship that exists between a person and his or her environment can blind us to the reality of systemic sin. Erickson argues that

> the particular social situation in which we involuntarily find ourselves—including the political and economic system, our intellectual and family background, even the geographical location in which we were born—inevitably contributes to evil conditions and in some instances makes sin unavoidable. Sin is an element of the present social structure from which the individual cannot escape.[93]

He sees the solution as a call for personal repentance and a movement toward nonviolent reform.[94] People need to come to personal faith in Jesus Christ and work through peaceful means to institute justice. The church itself provides an opportunity to model such a course of action.

We in the church are hindered by many things, but in light of our individualistic tendencies, one phenomenon is particularly telling. When we read certain passages from Scripture, the immediate thought is how it applies to "me" and not necessarily to "me" as part of a living, vital organism, the church of Jesus Christ. A believer could read 1 Peter 2:9—"But you are a chosen people, a royal priesthood, a holy nation, a people belonging to God. . . ."—and immediately conclude, "I am a priest." This is true of course, but the plural nature of the statement could go unnoticed, with damaging consequences. Reflection upon the "I" as a part of the whole immediately raises the consciousness to interpersonal dynamics and the rules that govern how people relate to one another. This enhanced community consciousness would aid in identifying and appreciating the fact of systemic sin because it gets our eyes off ourselves.

3
What Is the Future of Black Theology?

J. Deotis Roberts, in the preface to *Black Theology in Dialogue,* states a view held by many in the black theological community that, "Black theology has come of age. It is now a dialogue partner with theological developments around the world. . . . Black theology is a dialogue partner with theological developments worldwide."[1]

James Cone observes in *Black Theology: A Documentary History, Volume Two: 1980–1992* that the second generation of black theologians represented in the volume are characterized by a number of factors. For the purpose of this section, one characteristic immediately draws attention. It is the fact that this new generation does not see the need to defend their discipline to the larger white-dominated theological academy. They simply assume the right to do theology from their own perspective.[2] A healthy sign of development, however, is the capacity to entertain criticism from the outside and to undertake self-criticism from within. Consideration

71

of criticism is essential for black theology if there is any hope of its continued existence and relevance.

In an earlier work Cone identified four weaknesses of early black theology.[3] First, black theology gave the impression that its only reason for existence was a negative reaction to white racism rather than a result of the positive elements of black culture and theological reflection. Second, there was an inadequate use of the social sciences to analyze the situation confronting the formulation of a viable black theology. Cone suggests that the community did not adequately explore the relationships "between racism, capitalism and imperialism, on the one hand, and theology and the church on the other."[4] Such explorations, for example, would have revealed the futility of Martin Luther King Jr.'s initial appeal to the conscience of the nation regarding the historical and contemporary dehumanization of black Americans. Social reflection of a more informed nature would have shown more fully the depth of the relationship between personal and institutional racism.

Third, Cone focused on a lack of economic analysis as a weakness in early black theology. Marxism, in his view, would be a helpful tool in the process of liberation because it would confront black preachers and theologians with the dynamics of class struggles in a national community. This resultant awareness would in turn inhibit the possibility of black leaders preaching liberation while fleecing the flock, something that is possible because of the influence of capitalism in American culture. Finally, early black theology was plagued by inadequate gender analysis. Cone recognizes that "black theologians and ministers, men and women, have major problems to face in the church and the society."[5] There are significant connections between the effects of racism and the manifestations of sexism in black society and in the black church.

Self-criticism is, without doubt, a sign of maturity in the discipline of black theology. My remaining commentary, however, is not intended to respond point-by-point to Cone's critique. I have concerns that in some ways correspond to his concerns. My concerns, however, stem from two possible scenarios that arise from allowing experience to have the foundational interpretive role for theological formulation. Experience, apart from the transcendent perspective of revelation as embodied in Scripture and practiced in the community yielded to Scripture, cannot itself be evaluated. It simply rules in this interpretive role just as those with the loudest voices or most persuasive rhetoric may gain the position of defining what genuine life should look like in a given community. One possible resultant scenario is for black theological reflection to degenerate to something more in line with sociology that is merely baptized with Christian terminology. The other is to forsake Christian foundations altogether in the name of developing a liberating theology. The third and ideal scenario is to maintain the foundations of biblical truth while exploring the implications for the faith regarding matters of justice, humanization, and community.

Ronald Potter, while directing his comments primarily to black evangelicals, raises a needed concern for black theology in general. He calls for a continued grounding in Scripture. "Without the Scripture as a norm, all God-talk drops to the level of humanism and anthropology."[6] William Bentley expresses a similar concern. While black theologians cannot be overly individualistic on the ramifications of the gospel so as to neglect its social significance, they must not "be so blinded by some elements of our cultural heritage, that we in effect identify the Gospel with our Black culture."[7]

Anthony Pinn represents a move toward forsaking foundational Christian tradition, long held in the African-American church. Rather than engaging in the traditional theodicy issue that attempts to formulate a rationale for historical and contemporary racism against African-Americans, Pinn argues for a questioning of God's existence altogether.[8] He unashamedly challenges the logic of continuing to embrace long-held religious doctrine that he believes hinders the liberation struggle. The echoes of Martin Luther's stand at the Diet of Worms (1521) resound in one of Pinn's opening statements:

> I believe that human liberation is more important than the maintenance of any religious symbol, sign, canon, or icon. It must be accomplished—both psychologically and physically—despite the damage done to cherished religious principles and traditions. Holding to this belief, I will stand or fall.[9]

I can appreciate and respect Pinn's fervor and his burden to alleviate human suffering, but there is a need for further reflection here. Though I will address some issues more thoroughly later in this chapter, a number of questions immediately arise when considering an experience-based ideology and liberation strategy. What does "liberation" mean and what should it look like? How would we recognize it? What are the reasons for Pinn's confidence that oppressed people can achieve such liberation without a view of, or reliance on, God? Who or what will govern the oppressed community if and when liberation is achieved? What comprises the moral and ethical imperative that would compel those outside of the African-American community to hear and heed the call for such liberation?[10]

Many needs confront the African-American community and there are also issues of oppression in many other lands at present. Seemingly insurmountable problems such as broken families, promiscuity, teen pregnancy, drugs, gangs, rage, and hopelessness[11] exist in desperate proportions.

In order to be a viable force for the advancement of the African-American community and to maintain its viability, black theology must contribute to a resolution of these matters. It cannot exist as mere academic investigation and rhetoric. To that end, four areas of black theology must be continually evaluated: (1) its relationship to Christian tradition; (2) the question of hermeneutics; (3) its relationship to the larger theological community; and (4) the danger of losing its Christian identity.

Black Theology's Relationship with Christian Tradition

Black theology's relationship with Christian tradition begins with and is perpetuated through the black church. By the term *Christian tradition* I mean basic beliefs about God, the Bible, Jesus Christ, the church, and appropriate living before God and others.[12] I reaffirm here what I stated in the first chapter: many voices provide testimony to the foundational nature of the black church for the African-American community and black theology. While the foundation can be affirmed or criticized, the connection to the black church is undeniable. Some in the church, who are willing to interact with and respond to black theology, reflect a tradition in line with evangelical perspectives. Joseph Jackson, after stating core doctrinal beliefs on God, Christ, and the nature of salvation, writes that he must reject

> any theologian, be he black or white, that limits the redemptive effort of Jesus Christ to any race, to any color, to any nationality or any rank or group in society [for he] denies and negates the positive principles of redemption as discussed above.[13]

Gayraud Wilmore sees Jackson's position, however, as a manifestation of the "Negro church," a church devoid of its historic liberative consciousness and mission.[14]

Wilmore and others argue that the liberation thrust of the gospel is biblical and grounded in the historical black church. Convictions such as those shown by Jackson reveal the "ghost of the culturally irrelevant, fundamentalistic 'Negro' church of the early twentieth century. . . ."[15] Cone acknowledges that "everything I am as well as what I know that I ought to be was shaped in the context of the black church." Simultaneously, he warns that unless the black community applies rigorous economic and political analysis to the church communities and calls for repentance for its widespread inertia in the struggle for liberation, it will remain a "relic of history and nothing more."[16] Dennis Wiley holds that the black church and black theology can engage in a symbiotic relationship, each contributing to the life and mission of the other.

James Evans demonstrates a profound grasp of the nature of ecclesiastical statements when he writes that they are "contested" statements. They are contested because of the complexities involved in describing the relationship between the human and the divine, a topic inherent to any discussion on the nature and mission of the church.[17] He then argues for a "liberative" definition of the church:

> Liberation has been central to the African-American churches' self-understanding since its inception. This liberation, however, is not just the missiological thrust of the church, it is the essence of the church's identity. Liberation is not just what the church *does*; it is what the church *is*. . . . If human liberation is seen as central to the life of the church, then to lose sight of that center is to relinquish its claim to be the church.[18]

Liberation must inculcate a freedom for the individual and the community from which the individual comes. The self does not exist apart from community, and community is comprised of a body of conscious, responsible individuals. Liberation is not achieved if only one element, that is, one individual or community, is free. Evans argues that Jesus is the center of the church, that the *kerygma* is the theological reason for the church's existence, and that the church is sustained through the power of the Spirit.[19] All of these essential aspects enable the church to be "that community which serves the cause of freedom and love in the world."[20]

The concerns expressed by these pastor-theologians are worthy of much more scrutiny, certainly much more than I can offer here. There are, however, a number of issues I will address before the end of this chapter. For instance, the implications of the nature of the black church and the mission derived from this defining comprehension must be identified. The relationship between the black church and what is understood as Christian tradition is a matter crucial for the sustenance of identity and life for the African-American community. The prominence of the church in the life of the African-American community has been overwhelmingly established. What will affect the future of black theology is its continuity or discontinuity with the black church. The black church can be said to be a church only insofar as it is identified with historical-biblical Christian doctrine. This point cannot be easily contested. Historical-biblical doctrine defines the church, the redeemed in Jesus Christ. Any other definition is a product of other sources or other authorities.

Wiley's statement is demonstrative of the need to recall the nature and mission of the church:

> Generally speaking, Black theology, as a conscious, rational, and disciplined attempt to reinterpret the gospel of Jesus Christ in light of the inner, as well as the outer, oppression of African-American people has never been a widespread phenomenon within the Black Church.[21]

This is a telling statement for two reasons. First, it relates that the type of systemization that is presently being done in much of black theology has not been a dominant practice in the church. Related to this is the realization that other points of belief and application had to be occupying the attention of the black church. Reflection on what constitutes true belief, that which is foundational to what the church is and what the church should be doing, also held attention. It is simply unacceptable to defend black theology by merely pointing to the imposition of belief on the black church by slave-traders, Eurocentric theologians, and possible "Uncle Toms" in the church itself. There is a network of beliefs that makes a church Christian as opposed to other religious forms or types of sociocultural institutions. The misapplication of a doctrine does not, in and of itself, make the doctrine untrue, Eurocentric, or enslaving.[22]

The church, black or white, is the church because of adherence to certain truths correctly held as transcendent, normative, and authoritative. Such a belief system inherently encompasses beliefs about the nature of God, Scripture, Jesus Christ, humanity, and the Holy Spirit. My purpose at this point, as well as in the rest of this chapter, is not to delineate a doctrinal statement, though I will be further addressing some doctrinal issues. Suffice it to say that the black church historically has scrutinized the meaning of the gospel in ways other than physical, economic, political, and cultural liberation. These reflections on belief and life, because of their transcendent nature, speak to concerns such as: What does freedom or liberation mean and how will it be achieved? Are we left with interpretations of reality that are only the product of our experiences? If experience is ultimate, what is the nature of any moral imperative that seeks to describe and move toward conditions as they should exist? Black theology's moral imperative has been and always will be authoritative in the African-American community and outside the community only in proportion to its faithfulness to Scripture as mediated in and through the black church. This raises the question of hermeneutics.

The Question of Hermeneutics

Biblical hermeneutics is the interpretation and application of the biblical text. Though there may be other texts in a given culture deserving of some interpretation, the focus in the black church and for black theology is Scripture. The methodology of the interpreter is critically determinative, not only for the meaning of the text, but also for theological formulation.[23] Of course, many factors affected the compilation of the biblical text and the ways that it was interpreted and applied throughout the history of the church. There are factors that bear upon the interpreter as he or she seeks meaning in the text and determines what should be stressed in theological reflection. Discussion of these factors is beyond the scope of this present work. Suffice it to argue that the identification and analysis of some common practices in hermeneutics as implemented in black theology cuts to the heart of the future of black theology. If future study accomplishes both the construction of a sociocultural liberative theology and the faithful adherence to the basic doctrinal beliefs that make the black church a church, then black theology will have a future in the black church, in academia, and in the broad spectrum of sociocultural communities.

Anthony Thiselton correctly observes three common characteristics that the hermeneutic of black theology shares with liberation and feminist theologies. First, their hermeneutic calls for a critique of the interpretive frameworks of dominant theological traditions. These hermeneutical frameworks are part of a network of pre-understandings that prescribe what should be understood and applied from the biblical texts. However, the teaching is understood and applied in a way that only allows conditions to continue as they were, with those in power remaining in power. An interpretive framework that allows an individual or a community to see in Scripture only the Jesus "meek and mild," for example, does not lend itself to confronting injustice and dehumanization.

Second, like the other theological systems, a black biblical hermeneutic offers a reinterpretation of the texts from the standpoint of the oppressed. The oppressed community studies Scripture to meet God and determine his will for their lives. The intent of study is to derive a hope and a plan for justice and humanization. The hermeneutics of dominant traditions, it is argued, will not facilitate this vision of liberation. Third, a black biblical hermeneutic intentionally seeks critical tools to expose the use of biblical texts by the dominant traditions as a means to serve the "social interests of domination, manipulation, or oppression."[24] It is extremely important within this sphere of study to adopt a critical position when confronting the teaching from the biblical text as propounded by present prevailing powers in biblical and theological study.

The primary question confronting any black hermeneutic is whether the members of the interpretive community are engaging in a sociocritical or a sociopragmatic approach. Thiselton defines a sociocritical hermeneutic as "an approach to texts (or to traditions and institutions) which seeks to penetrate beneath their surface-function *to expose their role as instruments of power, domination, or social manipulation.*"[25] The intent of a sociocritical hermeneutic is to formulate a transcendent perspective that is distinct from the texts or the traditions under scrutiny. Through the attainment of such a perspective, any manipulation of texts to perpetuate various forms of oppression would be exposed. This transcendent perspective may, in turn, confront the interpretive community on a number of fronts.

A sociopragmatic hermeneutic, however, functions only within the confines of a given tradition. Such a system can make no legitimate claim to a critical stance that could criticize and compel response from a dominant, oppressive tradition. It functions authoritatively only in its own community. Thiselton poses questions that are relevant not only to a black hermeneutic, but also to any system that proclaims a search for structural, institutional justice:

> Do the hermeneutical systems constructed or utilized by liberation theologies or by feminist approaches function *pragmatically to filter out from the biblical text* any signal which does anything other than affirm the hopes and aspirations of a given social group; or to do they embody a *genuine sociocritical principle which unmasks oppression as part of a larger trans-contextual critique?* Do they merely reflect back the horizons of the community of protest in self-affirmation, or

do they offer a social critique under which all (or many) communities may experience correction, transformation, and enlargement of horizons?[26]

Without consistent identification and implementation of a transcendent perspective in black biblical hermeneutics, there is no "command" to change the dominant social, political, economic, and theological structures. The resultant theological formulation can only speak to the black interpretive community. That may be sufficient for some. The cost, however, is too dear for those who want to prove convincing to other communities and work effectively for change. This prophetic role could be a perpetual legacy of black theology.

Though not popular in terms of biblical hermeneutics, the goal of approximating the intent of the biblical writers would be a helpful standard for comparing interpretations of the text and for validating authoritative teaching. Despite suspicions of latent power structures in the written text, the text will simply become the power construct of the reader. The interpretation of the community's experience, whether individual or corporate, can itself never be tested or evaluated. A person's or community's claims about God, Jesus Christ, and the mission of the church could never be evaluated. As I mentioned above, a sociopragmatic implementation of Scripture may serve well the purpose of a particular community. Such an approach, however, can never build bridges of understanding between communities.

Black Theology's Relationship with the Larger Theological Community

Some voices in the black theological community argue that they need not be concerned about the standards for credible theological formulation as set forth by the dominant Eurocentric biblical and theological community. Cone, for example, argues that in light of the centrality of the black experience in the development of black theology, it "must take seriously the questions which arise from black-existence and not even try to answer white questions, questions coming from the lips of those who know oppressed existence only through abstract reflections."[27]

James Evans sees the need for an interplay of the "canonical" story of the Bible with the "folk" story of African-Americans. Black theologians, then,

> must tell a story that relates the hope of the biblical message with the realism of black experience. Through the arrangement and explication of the basic Christian doctrines, from creation to consummation, black theologians must fashion a story that brings together the twin commitment of African-American Christians to faith and freedom.[28]

George Cummings observes that first generation black theologians such as Cone, Roberts, and Wilmore outlined structures for criticizing "white Christian institutions and religions" while declaring emancipation from their white Christian counterparts. Their accomplishment was the construction of a theology that was accountable primarily to the black experience.[29]

An analysis of the question of black theology's relationship with the broader theological community demands consideration of many factors. I will use two questions as methodological keys to unlock some of the issues involved. First, in what sense are black theologians free from the restraints of the dominant theological community? Second, if they do reject the voice of the dominant white theological presence in the name of synthesizing a relevant black theology, then how can black theologians affect change in the theology and the sociocultural attitudes of the dominant culture?

Since the days of the slave trade, the black church was affected by the Christianity of the dominant Western European culture. There were profound contributions from African worldviews and expressions of worship, but the black church was not free from the religious thought of the en-slavers.[30] Determinative themes in Christianity were, and are, foundational to the black church. Wherever one stands on the matter of the infusion of African religion, the influence of the dominant Christian culture was evident.

Many proponents of black theology were trained in pre-dominately white theological institutions. Such training may result in a type of "plunder[ing] of the Egyptians" (to use the words of Exodus 12:36), but an influence is still exerted. Training affects theological reflection through the use of ter-minology, concepts, and performance standards. Traditional theological language is still incorporated into black theo-logical discourse. To varying degrees the terms reflect the conceptual framework of the educating institution. In order to obtain a degree some type of standard of acceptability is involved. If an institution can influence terms, concepts, and standards, it can govern much of what one does in future reflections.

Some in the black theological community are presently attempting to derive these theological categories from a more definitive African context. Cummings, for example, sees slave narratives as giving

> ample testimony to the genius of African-American slaves, who combined the traditional African religions and Chris-tianity into a religio-cultural resource that transformed their brute cultural encounters with raw and meaningless suffer-ing into an experience of hope.[31]

He further associates the dominant African concepts of God and creation with the Christian convictions on Christ and the Spirit, particularly in the realm of God's liberating activ-ity on behalf of the oppressed.[32]

Those who identify with the black theological community must continue in the research, synthesis, and application of biblical and theological principles. All fields of study, of course, can contribute to this endeavor. Black theology, however, faces some unique challenges if it wishes to perpetuate the teaching and appropriation of liberative themes in our sociocultural setting, particularly in the realm of theological reflection. On the one hand, there exists a widespread concern to do theology relevant to the needs of the African-American community, with the church as focal to this community. On the other hand, to have a hope of impacting the larger theological community, some prerequisites exist. The task of ongoing biblical and theological study, with relevant accompanying disciplines, is an incessant call.

The black theological community must also be willing to accept criticism from those considered outside the liberation community, even those who through latent, and sometimes obvious, racism, patriarchy, and homophobia, may be involved in perpetuating dehumanization and structural oppression for African-Americans. In order to develop persuasive dogma, that is, authoritative instruction, other factors may require attention. Such factors include internal consistency within the discipline of black theology. When God is mentioned by a member of the community, for example, is he or she talking about the same God referred to by other members of the community? If a consensus exists, how was it attained? Have there been debates concerning sources or agreed applications? Has a view of God been declared heretical? What role should Scripture have in theological synthesis and the evaluation of such syntheses? The same types of questions could be posed about any area of theology.

These types of issues may seem superfluous to many in the black theological community, especially when set against the backdrop of the urgent need for liberation here and now. However, conversion of "outsiders" to such a perspective may demand more attention to such questions. Whether it is appreciated or not, the bodies of theological reflection that confront black theology are often affected by centuries of dogmatic development, and thus they cannot be easily bypassed in the name of a desperate call for liberation. Questions could be legitimately raised about the meaning of liberation, the authorities cited for such meaning, and why those of another theological perspective should listen to the oppressed. Engagement according to the acceptable standards of those in power must be considered for the sake of persuasion.

Does this require the forsaking of confrontational and liberative themes? I would strongly deny such a conclusion. In no way do I desire to create the impression that matters of justice and the related affirmation of African-American humanity must be sacrificed in order to construct an "acceptable" theology. I am only concerned with the matter of what is required to be persuasive to the larger theological community, at least as a start toward the wider sociocultural community. I will have more to say on this matter at the end of the chapter.

Black theologians must be very adept at identifying the core beliefs in Christianity that may be considered abstract and thus difficult to understand or apply. They should also be aware of violations and inconsistent applications of numerous Christian principles on the part of some people. Problems connected with the latter are not necessarily characteristic of the former. Serious challenges to and reformulation of core beliefs will position black theology away from orthodox faith, inhibiting its contribution to the African-American church and community and eventually ushering it into nonexistence.

The Danger of Losing a "Christian" Identity

What is Christianity? What content does the label Christian have? What should it have? Are we free to give the term any meaning that we find advantageous? Is there a line that one can cross where the resultant beliefs can no longer be considered Christian? Certain beliefs comprise the core of Christianity; without adherence to these central doctrines Christianity no longer exists.

Though he is not addressing the content of Christian belief directly, Alister McGrath offers a warning to black theologians who may run the danger of using Christian tradition and terminology to advance a sociopolitical agenda. If long-held doctrine is sufficiently modified or redefined, the resultant system may be conducive for a particular understanding of liberation; but, McGrath asks, "Does such an understanding actively enable us to commend Christianity to others? What is the motivation for evangelism in this context? What is it about the Christian story that commends it above other stories?"[33]

Doctrinal distinctives must be maintained in order to accomplish three things. First, they authorize the use of the descriptive term, *Christian*. Second, they enhance the hope of motivating others who share elements of Christian dogma to consider more fully what it means "to act justly and to love mercy and to walk humbly with your God" (Micah 6:8). Finally, they will assist the African-American church in ministry to the African-American community, as well as to the church in general.

My purpose here is not to discuss all doctrines that are worthy of research and application. My goal is to encourage reflection on a representative number of significant doctrines that will inspire attention to others. Maintaining a Christian identity is central in my discussion of some recent developments in black theology in the doctrines of God, the atonement, humanity, and salvation. A foundational Christian identity is the only thing that will insure the future of black theology as a viable contributor to the African-American church and ultimately to the African-American community.

God

James Cone exhibits a pervasive conviction about the portrayal of God in Christian theology:

I believe that Christian theology is language about God. But it's more than that, and it is the 'more' that makes theology

Christian. Christian theology is language about the *liberating* character of God's presence in Jesus Christ as he calls his people into being for freedom in the world.[34]

God is overwhelmingly concerned with freedom from institutional and other structural oppression. Sin is then largely an affront to human beings in the form of attitudes and practices that enable oppressors to view others as somehow inferior and to treat them accordingly. There is a desire on the part of the Divine that people, African-Americans in particular because of their situation in the American sociocultural context, experience liberation from dehumanizing dynamics. God demonstrates a preference for the poor and the oppressed, and this preference makes up the essence of the gospel of Jesus Christ.

As already shown in the first chapter, the exodus tradition has been used as proof of God's response against social and political oppression. Offering a commentary on Exodus 19:4–5a, Cone states, "By delivering this people from Egyptian bondage and inaugurating the covenant on the basis of that historical event, God reveals that he is the God of the oppressed, involved in their history, liberating them from human bondage."[35] Biblical testimony, particularly in the prophets, supports the view of God as one adamantly opposed to injustice and enslavement. Amos, for example, thunders against the practice of slavery, a decisive paradigm of dehumanization:

> This is what the LORD says: "For three sins of Gaza, even for four, I will not turn back my wrath. Because she took captive whole communities and sold them to Edom . . . For three sins of Tyre, even for four, I will not turn back my wrath. Because she sold whole communities of captives to Edom, disregarding a treaty of brotherhood." (Amos 1:6, 9)

Those who bind themselves to the Lord God to live according to his ways make justice a priority because, "I, the LORD, love justice; I hate robbery and iniquity. In my faithfulness I will reward them and make an everlasting covenant with them" (Isa. 61:8).[36]

Many other passages could be cited to demonstrate God's demand for justice on behalf of the powerless and the special attention he gives to them. Cone and others are right in this regard. But other characteristics of the God of the exodus must be considered, otherwise the emerging picture of God is one of a mere force for change and relationship with this force degenerates into a social program. Such a view borders on idolatry.

The God who is portrayed in the canonical texts, however, is also a God who demands obedience, especially from those who are called "my treasured possession" (Exod. 19:5) and "his people" (Deut. 7:6).[37] From an early period in their existence as a nation, the people of Israel were warned not to forget the Lord their God:

> Be careful that you do not forget the LORD your God, failing to observe his commands, his laws and his decrees that I am giving you this day. Otherwise, when you eat and are satisfied, when you build fine houses and settle down, and when your herds and flocks grow large and your silver and gold increase and all you have is multiplied, then your heart will become proud and you will forget the LORD your God, who brought you out of Egypt, out of the land of slavery. (Deut. 8:11–14)

Peter Craigie correctly suggests that Israel deliberately failed to keep God's "commandments, judgments, and statutes" because the truth of God was in their minds but not in their hearts.[38]

The idea of a call to particular attitudes and behavior is reflected for the Christian church in the New Testament through exhortations and commands. I realize that the issue of sociocultural influences on exegesis is intimately involved in determining the meaning and force of these passages, but their presence confronts any proponent of biblical teaching with calls to particular standards of thought and behavior. Some things were to be believed—"Jesus is the Christ, the Son of God" (John 20:31). Some attitudes were to be adopted—"clothe yourselves with compassion, kindness, humility, gentleness and patience" (Col. 3:12). Certain behavior was unacceptable—"It is God's will that you should be sanctified: that you should avoid sexual immorality" (1 Thess. 4:3). In other words, God demands appropriate perspective and practice from those who are in special relationship with him.

The people of God never had total freedom to define or redefine the form and content of appropriate perspective and practice. There was some freedom, but constant words of caution were also present. No claims to charismatic gifts could remove the believers from various demands. A classic case in point is the message to the seven churches in Revelation 2–3. I will not go into particulars at this point, other than to point out that the churches, for the most part, were credited for some things, but admonished about others. God still had standards.

The God who demands also makes provision for his own in order that they are equipped to obey.[39] Human incapacity was factored into the covenantal relationships, calling for radical transformation. Jeremiah 31:33 suggests such a transformation when the God of Israel says, "I will put my law in their minds and write it on their hearts." This passage is also cited in Hebrews 8 and 10, referring to the church. This is to say that God demands obedience and facilitates obedience for those who trust in him. His grace is needed by all regardless of gender, class, or race. No party stands approved before God simply by membership in one or more of these categories. Membership in the covenant community of the people of God requires faith in Jesus Christ to actualize rebirth (John 3:3) and adoption into God's family (Rom. 8:15–16).

The Atonement

A survey of doctrinal history quickly alerts us to the fact that there have been various interpretations of the nature and effects of the atonement. The atonement, an essential element of the work of Christ,[40] refers to the meaning and significance of Christ's death on the cross. A historical treatment of all proposed views is beyond the scope of this present work, though many surveys are available,[41] and the extent or the purpose of the atonement will not be discussed.[42] My primary concern is the way some in the black theological community, particularly in the area of womanist theology,[43] ascribe certain meanings to the cross. I want to briefly consider a couple of these interpretations before presenting some non-negotiables that must be maintained if the resultant view of the atonement is to remain Christian.

Cone affirms that the cross of Jesus was instrumental in the overcoming of "the power of sin, death, and Satan, thereby bestowing upon us the freedom to struggle against suffering which destroys humanity."[44] The cross as a demonstration of God's solidarity with the oppressed is an axiomatic element of his reflection on the meaning of the cross:

> The cross of Jesus reveals the extent of God's involvement in the suffering of the weak. God is not merely sympathetic with the social pain of the poor but becomes totally identified with them in their agony and pain. The pain of the oppressed is God's pain, for God takes their suffering as God's own, thereby freeing them from its ultimate control of their lives. . . . God in Christ became the Suffering Servant and thus took the humiliation and suffering of the oppressed into God's own history. This divine event that happened on the cross liberated the oppressed to fight against suffering while not being determined by it.[45]

This twofold view of the cross as the overcoming of personal and cosmological enemies and as the demonstration of solidarity with humanity has much merit in terms of biblical teaching. Colossians 2:15 gives the cross a victorious significance that encompasses realms other than mundane spacetime relationships.[46] Romans 5:8 shows God's advocacy for sinners, and Romans 6:4 speaks of death and new life that comes through a union with Christ. Despite Cone's foundational views on the nature and meaning of the atonement, I feel that he does not extend it far enough.

Cone's definition of the cross robs the cross of both its endurance of suffering force and its substitutionary nature. As I intimated above, I do not wish to suggest that there is not a multiplicity of meanings properly proposed for the single event of Christ's death on the cross. I am arguing that some understandings lie outside of biblical parameters, and are therefore non-Christian. Not all interpretations of the atonement offered in the name of constructing a relevant understanding of the event and driven by a unique set of experiences may be called Christian.

Delores Williams, against the backdrop of black women's experience of "surrogacy," argues that many of the traditional views regarding the nature of the atonement place Jesus in a surrogate role.[47] He is one who has taken the place of others on the cross. Williams has great concern that the idea of this surrogacy on the part of Jesus may be regarded as a "sacred" substitution with an accompanying "sacred" aura then surrounding suffering. She surmises a real dilemma for black women in relationship to this surrogate-like understanding of the atonement:

> It is therefore fitting and proper for black women to ask whether the image of a surrogate-God has salvific power for black women or whether this image supports and reinforces the exploitation that has accompanied their experience with surrogacy. If black women accept this idea of redemption, can they not also passively accept the exploitation that surrogacy brings?[48]

According to Williams, the suffering and death of Jesus on the cross cannot have redemptive force for black women because that would be a type of baptism of their own suffering through the evil of surrogacy. Williams argues that "there is nothing divine in the blood of the cross."[49] Rather, the cross represents the evil response of human principalities and powers to the *ministerial*[50] vision of Jesus. Jesus came to reveal a way of "righting relations between body (individual and community), mind (of humans and of tradition) and spirit."[51]

Williams argues her case for the atonement not only on the basis of black women's experience, but also on the basis of observations drawn from the realm of doctrinal history. She cites the examples of Origen (185–254), Anselm (1033–1109), Abelard (1079–1142), and Calvin (1509–1564) as those who formulated their views of the atonement as the result of the sociopolitical environment in which they lived.[52] Similarly, there is then justification for her view of the atonement as the product of the unique needs of black women because it is the manifestation of human opposition to Jesus' ministerial vision.

In response to Williams's proposal, three things require attention. First, the doctrine of the atonement as constructed by Origen and others was not only the product of the sociopolitical surroundings in which they lived. There were other factors. Second, they incorporated biblical models in their view of the atonement. From the perspective of Scripture, it is difficult to maintain that the cross was simply the manifestation of evil human reaction to the *ministerial* vision of Jesus. Demarest captures well the relationship between Christ and the cross: "Christianity is Christ, and the crucial fact about Christ is his passion on the cross. Christ's example, teachings, and miracles must not be neglected by the inquirer into truth; but his atoning death is absolutely crucial."[53] Though Williams's focus on the *life* of Christ, as affirmed partially by Demarest, has much to contribute to christological reflection, it seems shortsighted. In Matthew 20:28, for example, it is difficult to separate the life and death of Christ.[54] Teaching that the basis for greatness was service,

Jesus encapsulates his ministry by teaching that he came to serve *and* to give his life a ransom for many. It is difficult to separate the significance of Jesus' death from the significance of his life.[55]

Third, the historical theologians cited as examples undoubtedly understood, in light of biblical teaching, that what brings about blessings for people who believe in Jesus is his death on the cross. The death of Christ was the facilitation of grace, mercy, and peace. For Origen, Christ was paid as a ransom to Satan.[56] Anselm believed that Christ's death was a substitutionary payment made to God to effect an appeasement of his honor. Abelard held that Christ's death was a demonstration of the love of God because "it was humans' fear and ignorance of God that needed to be rectified. This was accomplished by Christ's death."[57] Calvin emphasized the death of Christ in the matter of substitutionary atonement.

Sociocultural dynamics were not the only factors that played a role in the development of historical theories of the atonement. Sociocultural environment did have an effect upon their expression, but they never deviated from the focal point of Christ's death. From a biblically and historically theological perspective, then, Williams's interpretation of the atonement is highly problematic. Any appeal to experience opens the door to any formulation of the atonement or other important doctrines if it is deemed necessary to meet needs as they are interpreted through experience.

Robert Letham outlines a biblical-theological framework into which any offering on the nature and meaning of the atonement must fit.[58] I will allude only to those aspects that effectively reveal some foundational characteristics of his theological framework: penal substitution, reconciliation, conquest, and moral example.

The admissibility of penal substitution as a legitimate interpretation of the atonement has long been debated in the history of the church. It incorporates some considerations that have proven to be very distasteful. Nevertheless, the issue of

Christ enduring punishment on behalf of humanity must draw attention. Letham correctly observes that "the obvious questions that arise from this claim relate to the nature of the penalty and the one who exacts it."[59] God's law has been broken and the penalty for sin is death (Rom. 6:23). The idea of substitution alerts us to the fact that Christ took the place of human beings who deserved to pay the penalty for themselves. Though potentially raising the question of God's fairness in all this, the New Testament gives clear teaching on this view of the atonement. Second Corinthians 5:21a reads, "God made him who had no sin to be sin for us." Similarly, the writer of Hebrews says, "So Christ was sacrificed once to take away the sins of many people" (9:28a). Though aspects of this view of the atonement may pose problems for some, alternate understandings encounter problems as well. Letham wisely provides another needed reflection: "Problems arise when the atonement is analyzed in detachment from the frame of reference that the Bible gives it. It can then seem a cold, almost heartless, business transaction."[60] This point is significant for the development of biblical convictions on the atonement.

Reconciliation is a term that can be full of beauty and peace. Meditation on the significance of the atonement will arouse a sense of beauty and peace only when it is seen as the basis for reconciliation in the Bible. Second Corinthians 5:18 introduces us to a foundational element in biblical reconciliation. Vorlander and Brown argue that God is the subject or initiator of reconciliation, and as such, "The *katallage* [reconciliation] created by God is thus a completed act which precedes all human action."[61] Letham makes plain that it is Jesus Christ and his work on the cross that effects reconciliation:

This reconciliation is discussed in several places in the New Testament, chiefly by Paul. In Romans 5:10–11 he locates our reconciliation to God at the point of Christ's death, and looks forward to its ultimate consummation when Christ returns.[62]

Colossians 1:19–20 provides a broader, cosmological perspective on the reality of reconciliation that is still effected, however, by the cross of Christ.

Any view that seeks to synthesize Scripture with reconciliation must factor in the atonement. It is the foundation for real peace with God and reconciliation among human beings, as God moves to restore harmony in all of creation (Rom. 8:19–21).

Related to this cosmological aspect of reconciliation is Letham's view of Christ's death as a conquest of "the rebellious principalities and powers, the demonic world headed by Satan."[63] This biblical perspective, Letham suggests, brings an enhanced awareness to some essential points. First, the death and resurrection of Christ are brought together into a rich harmony. Death is not the final word. The resurrection is a sign of the acceptability of Christ's death as an atoning sacrifice for the believer's sin and is also the assurance of the believer's resurrection into eternal life (1 Cor. 15:22–23). Second, we are reminded that full victory will not be accomplished until the Lord returns. Sin and Satan exert influence in the realm of time and space, but God's consummation is sure (1 Cor. 15:24–28). Third, Christ's conquest of sin and Satan empowers us to confront the human ills arising from these two thorns that have long plagued us. In life, Jesus Christ brought holistic healing to individuals (healing the leper's body [Matt. 8:3–4]; forgiving sin [Mark 2:5]; facilitating radical change in life [Luke 19:8–10]; overcoming the demonic [Mark 5:15]). I will briefly comment on this potential empowerment through a reflection on the Gerasene demoniac (Mark 5:1–20) as it relates to racism.

After citing a number of passages in the gospels speaking of demon possession, Millard Erickson correctly observes: "In all of these cases the common element is that the person involved is being destroyed, whether physically, emotionally, or spiritually."[64] He points out further that not all damage done to humans, whether physical, emotional, or spiritual, is done by demons. It is possible for human beings, however, to think and act demonically. Demons could be involved with humans, but humans are also perfectly capable of thinking and acting in a way that parrots the demonic. As the case of the Gerasene demoniac shows, demons desire to mar and destroy people who are image-bearers of God. Racism, which is a form of marring God's image-bearers, may be demonically inspired in some. This is a possibility that must be taken seriously by the church, and the conquest of Jesus must be prayerfully applied to the situations as they are confronted. Human beings can think and act demonically when a fellow image-bearer of God is regarded and treated as something inferior. Ironically, by participating in such behavior, the violator becomes less human.

It is one thing to identify the problem of racism, and a whole other issue to have power to overcome it. Only by faith in Jesus Christ, by becoming a new creation in him (2 Cor. 5:17), can there be a hope of overcoming racism. Christ's work on the cross is a manifestation of power and is the source for the hope of overcoming this and other human maladies.

Lest one be concerned about deliberations on the atonement that lead to theoretical, inactive conclusions, Letham also offers the atonement as moral example. He confesses that the atonement is exemplary only indirectly, but it does contribute to the model of patient, loving endurance that Jesus provided (1 Pet. 2:21–25).[65] Confrontation with evil may be costly and love does not automatically preclude confrontation. Divinely empowered endurance is needed to overcome the individual and systemic manifestations of sin in our sociocultural milieu. Jesus demonstrated this type of endurance in his unrelenting commitment to the Father's will, up to and including the road to Calvary.

The fate of black theology as a contributing discipline to the church lies in its willingness to maintain the biblical-theological framework of the atonement that the church has confessed for centuries. This is not to suggest that restatement or renewal of application are unnecessary. It is simply to insist that the interpretation of the African-American experience that calls for sacrificing the biblical pictures of the atonement will contribute to the demise of the African-American church and the discipline of black theology. The way of ultimate liberation is still found in and through the cross of Christ, which facilitates both a deeper dependence upon God and the hope of victory.

Humanity

I can recall recent news broadcasts where Rev. Jesse Jackson appeared at a predominantly black school and led the student body in a leader-response chant: "I am somebody." He would repeat it several times. The students appeared to be excited about the message, one with which I wholeheartedly concur. But a question immediately arose in my mind: What if there are voices and situations in day-to-day life that loudly proclaim, "Nevertheless, you are nobody! You can shout and chant all you want, but I (we) have power to impose our view upon you." How do African-Americans manage to believe in their worth and live accordingly? Is it simply a matter of believing despite the views of those in such positions of power, or is there more to it?

In fact there is a basis for affirming the full humanity of African-Americans, as well as all other members of the human race. The basis is the biblical affirmation that we are made in the image of God (*imago Dei*). It is not my intent to discuss the precise nature of the image, the effects of the fall and sin on it, or the nature of the restored image in Jesus Christ (Rom. 8:29).[66] Instead I want to explore the implications of two things: first, the fact that the source of such information is the Bible, and second, the fact that we are creatures defined in relationship with and belonging to God.

By way of the first implication, the Bible that reveals human beings are made in the image of God has other things to say about human nature. Second, our being made in the image of God sets boundaries upon our understanding of human freedom. We are inextricably bound to God for everything, particularly in the realm of what defines us as human beings. Emil Brunner suggests,

> As a creature "I" belong wholly to God; I am not independent and free, but I am a being who is derived from, and made for, God. This perception of what it means to be a "creature" does not deny our freedom, but it springs from the fact that our freedom is founded in God, and limited by [the fact] that . . . we cannot speak of our "creatureliness" without dealing at the same time with the truth that man has been created in the Image of God.[67]

The biblical reality of human beings created in the image of God (*imago Dei*) provides much motivation for liberative efforts to affirm and actualize the full humanity of all people. However, the application of what may be seen as liberation for some in the name of the *imago Dei* can be problematic. For example, some in the black theological community have been too quick to endorse the gay lifestyle. I realize that as soon as I mention this issue I will be charged with hatred, homophobia, and ignorance. It is not my intent to be hateful, nor is my concern to suggest that homosexuality is a worse transgression than the sexual sins of heterosexuals. It has more to do with the issues I raised above, namely, that if we allow the Bible to define us as image-bearers of God, we are confronted with other teachings from this same Bible that fill in the appropriate understanding of what it means for us to live as image-bearers. The Bible also alerts us to the fact that we are not free to define ourselves or behave in any way that we may see fit without running the serious risk of distorting who we are and what we should be doing in the Christian community. If the totality of the Bible's message is true, we would also run a greater risk of the Lord's disapproval.[68]

Against the backdrop of the call for a "holistic Black theology that integrates race, class, gender, sexual orientation, and ecological analyses,"[69] some black female religious academics have engaged in discussions concerning the gay community. Though it is not the only matter that Cheryl Sanders discusses, she expresses a similar concern about the validity of using Alice Walker's term "womanist" to describe black feminist reflections on theology and ethics.[70] "Walker's definition comprises an implicit ethics of moral autonomy, liberation, sexuality and love that is not contingent upon the idea of God or revelation."[71] Since God and revelation have long been foundational to the worldview of African-American Christians, it would be inconsistent to adopt a framework for theological reflection that marginalizes these basic elements. Sanders does not mention a fear of the Lord's disapproval, but she does express a concern for the black family:

> In my view there is a fundamental discrepancy between the womanist criteria that would affirm and/or advocate homosexual practice, and the ethical norms the black church might employ to promote the survival and wholeness of black families. It is problematic for those of us who claim connectedness to and concern for those two institutions. If black women's ethics is to be pertinent to the needs of our community, then at least some of us must be in a position to offer intellectual guidance to the church as the principal (and perhaps only remaining) advocate for marriage and family in the black community.[72]

At the core of these issues is the question of what constitutes a human being and what is the source for such definition. This in turn has much to say about what is appropriate behavior for the individual and the larger sociocultural setting.

Charges of hatred, intolerance, and insensitivity could still be raised. On the one hand, I can sympathize with the plight of members of the gay community who experience mistreatment.[73] On the other hand, to define a person by "preference" is to say there is essentially a claim to a "third gender" on the basis of preference or tendency, resulting in another race of people who must be guarded and embraced by all. On what basis is such a means of human definition authoritative? Are preference and tendency criteria that we want to use to define what a person is?

Of course if Scripture is ignored, marginalized, or reinterpreted, then any definition of what constitutes humanity is allowable. As I have mentioned above, while homosexual behavior is no worse than other sins,[74] neither is it that which defines personhood. Hays acknowledges the power of sexual drives, but stresses the need to keep them in perspective:

> Never within the canonical perspective does sexuality become the basis for defining a person's identity or for finding meaning and fulfillment in life. The things that matter are justice, mercy, and faith (Matt. 23:23). The love of God is far more important than any human love. Sexual fulfillment finds its place, at best, as a subsidiary good within this larger picture.[75]

Men and women are defined in relationship to God and his will as revealed in Scripture. The drive on the part of some in the black theological community to grant an almost separate category of humanity to members of the gay community arises from something other than the Bible and Christian tradition. If one is moved to argue that the Bible is of questionable authority on this issue because of patriarchal and homophobic tendencies, then on what basis is it a reliable aid in human definition and Christlike behavior? Further, why should it be consulted at all, for anything? The lens of experience is just that—a lens.[76]

The black church, like the church in general, is entrusted with the mission of discipleship (Matt. 28:18–20). This is an enormous task, though not insurmountable given dependence on the grace and power of God in the proclamation and modeling of the gospel. As part of his well-balanced and sensitive treatment of the matter of homosexuality, Richard Hays incorporates some aspects of his relationship with Gary, a Christian friend who was gay. In his final letter to Hays before dying of AIDS, Gary addressed the matter of discipleship:

> Are homosexuals to be excluded from the community of faith? Certainly not. But anyone who joins such a community should know that it is a place of transformation, of discipline, of learning, and not merely a place to be comforted or indulged.[77]

Words of comfort and encouragement may certainly be appropriate given certain circumstances. However, black theology will be able to perpetuate the black church if it does not identify with the tendency in our larger social context to grant a functional definition of personhood. Rather, it needs to maintain a transforming view of Christian discipleship in accordance with the prayerfully researched, unchanging dimensions of God's revealed will.

Salvation

The salvation issue can be expressed in the question of the Philippian jailer: "Sirs, what must I do to be saved?" (Acts 16:30). How is a person found right in the sight of God? Black theology places overwhelming emphasis on analysis of human oppression and on the call to action because God sides with the oppressed. Does a person become a member of the community of the redeemed simply because he or she is a member of the community of the oppressed? Will one be ushered into the presence of the Lord Jesus Christ after departing this life simply because he or she was a sociopolitical activist on behalf of the marginalized? According to some, at least, the answer would be yes.

However, right standing before God, contrary to the idea above, is accomplished through faith in Jesus Christ alone. The person who has the problem of sin and separation from God will be granted a "righteousness from God, apart from law" through faith in Christ (Rom. 5:21–22). Salvation is not by works, "so that no one can boast" (Eph. 2:9). With such attention given to action in black theology, I am deeply burdened by any appearance of works-righteousness, whereby a person may gain the understanding that it is through good works that he or she gains forgiveness from God and obtains new life with him.

I can appreciate the perspective of those who, like the apostle James, war against an inactive, dead faith:

> What good is it, my brothers, if a man claims to have faith but has no deeds? Can such faith save him? Suppose a brother or sister is without clothes and daily food. If one of you says to him, "Go, I wish you well; keep warm and well fed," but does nothing about his physical needs, what good is it? In the same way, faith by itself, if it is not accompanied by action, is dead. (James 2:14–17)

A faith that truly appropriates the grace of God through Jesus Christ will not rest without a striving to please God in every way possible. I have encountered the helpful statement in a number of places that "we are saved by faith alone, but saving faith is never alone." There is a supernatural balance that must be maintained in this matter of right relationship with God. All of our righteous deeds are as "filthy rags" (Isa. 64:6) before God, but by faith in Christ, the believer comes saying, "I have come to do your will, O God" (Heb. 10:7).

Conclusion

I have attempted a fair treatment of the foundations of black theology. Because of its brevity, this presentation does not do justice to the breadth and depth of the discipline. Nonetheless, I have argued that the discipline brings needed reminders and points of confrontation to the predominately white evangelical church in the United States. I have discussed several topics connected with the future of black theology and my basic premise is that unless black theology remains within the parameters of certain biblical and traditional confessions, its power will dissipate and it will be rendered ineffective as a servant to the black church in particular, and to the church in general. Some may hold that close proximity to traditional belief will lead to a blunting of black theology's liberative message and force. I must concede the fact that this is a possibility. I would insist, however, that it is not a necessity.

Even during the days of slavery, Frederick Douglass, a former slave and an outspoken abolitionist, showed an awareness of two types of Christianity. In speaking against the hypocrisy of the slaveholders' religion he specifies that,

> What I have said respecting and against religion, I mean strictly to apply to the *slaveholding religion* of this land, and with no possible reference to Christianity proper; for, between the Christianity of this land, and the Christianity of Christ, I recognize the widest possible difference—so wide, that to receive the one as good, pure, and holy, is of necessity to reject the other as bad, corrupt, and wicked. To be the friend of the one, is of necessity to be the enemy of the other.[78]

There is a real possibility that orthodox faith can be plumbed to provide a socially active stance with needed protective boundaries. In more recent days Bishop Desmond Tutu has spoken of the prophetic dimension of the gospel:

> My worry is that the Church has by and large been too quiescent, seemingly afraid to rock the boat too much. There are splendid and glorious exceptions, such as Archbishop Luwum who confronted the evil Amin with the demands of the Gospel of Jesus Christ, and paid for this courageous act with his life—or the experience of Cardinal Malula in Zaire. My concern is for the integrity of the Church of Jesus Christ. We must be seen to be motivated, not by political considerations, but by the imperatives of the Gospel, speaking out that evil is evil, whether perpetrated by black or white. The

Church must be willing to pay the price of its loyalty to its Lord and Master.[79]

A lack of balance in terms of what authentic Christianity should look like in the world occurs when any one race, class, or gender in the church becomes too provincial. There is insufficient dialogue over Scripture, tradition, and sociocultural and political analyses among members of the church from broader cultural and geographical areas. With a willingness to listen to various bodies in the church a balance between right confession and right living in the world can be accomplished.

Members of the black theological community must be willing to talk to those who represent a historical, traditional orthodoxy that to a certain degree still encompasses deeply prejudiced people. Reconciliation is not an easy, painless endeavor. I am not advocating that blacks or whites should forget the past and wear rose-colored glasses when looking at the present. Rather, I am advancing a particular way of exercising the memory.

Robert Schreiter states the needed principle, "*In forgiving, we do not forget, we remember in a different way.*"[80] Memory is an essential element of who and what we are as human beings that can potentially lead to either bitterness and anger or peaceful resolution and joy. Schreiter points out that often a process is required whereby shame and pain can be voiced to others so that together the healing process can be actualized.[81] African-American Christians should be allowed to express painful experiences among their white brothers and sisters, even in the context of theological and philosophical dialogue. Such dialogue will contribute to an evangelical understanding of the concerns that arise among the black theological community and why their confession is formulated the way it is. Whether the black theological community is willing to communicate with the white evangelical church is another question. As a confessing member of the latter community, I must admit that I do not know whether my brothers and sisters in this wing of the church are willing and able to listen.

Apart from forgiveness, reconciliation, and adherence to long-held biblical faith, black theology will not only be rendered ineffective, but the membership of the black theological community will become more and more like their oppressors.

Notes

Chapter 1: What Is Black Theology?

1. The community that I refer to is generally conservative white evangelicalism. I am not suggesting that I have a fundamental disagreement with their understanding of orthodoxy. I do, however, have differences with the ways that orthodoxy is expressed (or not expressed) in social, cultural, and political applications. I suggest a more precise definition of conservative evangelicalism in chapter 2.

2. James H. Cone and Gayraud S. Wilmore, eds. *Black Theology: A Documentary History, Volume One: 1966–1979* (Maryknoll, N.Y.: Orbis, 1979), p. 101. See this citation and its accompanying commentary in James H. Harris, *Pastoral Theology: A Black Church Perspective* (Minneapolis: Fortress, 1991), pp. 59–60.

3. James H. Cone, *A Black Theology of Liberation* (Philadelphia: Lippincott, 1970), p. 11.

4. J. Deotis Roberts, *Liberation and Reconciliation* (Maryknoll, N.Y.: Orbis, 1994), p. 11.

5. See Gayraud S. Wilmore's introduction in *Black Theology: A Documentary History, Volume Two: 1980–1992*, ed. James H. Cone and Gayraud S. Wilmore (Maryknoll, N.Y.: Orbis, 1993), pp. 79–84. For more detailed argument against oppression produced by homophobia, see Elias Farajaje-Jones, "Breaking Silence: Toward an In-the-Life Theology," in *Black Theology*, vol. 2, pp. 139–59.

6. At the time of this writing, the preferred designation of people of African descent in the United States is *African-American*. Throughout this work, however, I will use *black* and *African-American* interchangeably. This alternative use is reflected in contemporary literature on black theology.

7. Cone argues, "Christian theology is a theology of liberation. . . . This means that its sole reason for existence is to put into ordered speech the meaning of God's activity in the world, so that the community of the oppressed will recognize that their inner thrust for liberation is not only *consistent* with the gospel but *is* the gospel of Jesus Christ" (*Black Theology of Liberation*, p. 17 [Cone's emphasis]).

8. I am not seeking to undervalue the significance of skin color here. Historical and contemporary factors in the United States preclude any such attempt even if it were intended. Skin color emerged as a factor in race relations from the beginnings of this

country. Cone, speaking on the matter of blackness, correctly observes, "The formative culture of the colonies demeaned the African as a human being, by associating blackness, and thus black people, with evil; by denying the existence of an indigenous African culture and civilization; and by rejecting the notion that Africans had any idea of a Supreme Being, thereby condemning them to the state of God-forsakenness and justifying their continued enslavement and exploitation" (*Black Theology*, vol. 2, p. 30).

9. Cone, *Black Theology of Liberation*, p. 121.

10. Ibid., p. 213.

11. Cone writes on the nature of this demonstration of preference for the oppressed: "God not only fights for them but takes their humiliated condition upon the divine Person and thereby breaks open a new future for the poor, different from their past and present miseries" (James H. Cone, *God of the Oppressed* [Maryknoll, N.Y.: Orbis, 1997], p. 128).

12. Wilmore, "Introduction: Part IV—Black Theology and the Black Church," in *Black Theology*, vol. 1, p. 243.

13. Ibid., p. 242.

14. See "The Episcopal Address to the 40th Quadrennial General Conference of the African Methodist Episcopal Zion Church (Excerpt)," in *Black Theology*, vol. 1, p. 299.

15. NCBC Committee on Theological Prospectus, "National Committee of Black Churchmen," in *Black Theology*, vol. 1, p. 101.

16. Paulo Freire, *Pedagogy of the Oppressed* (New York: Continuum, 1970), p. 28. Freire further argues that there is a need for a pedagogy of the oppressed that does not treat them as unfortunates or encourage them to search the oppressors for models. The oppressed must be their own models in the struggle for justice (p. 39). A liberating pedagogy will help to create a "new man." This new creation is required because, "If the goal of the oppressed is to become fully human, they will not achieve their goal by merely reversing the terms of the contradiction (oppressed-oppressor relationships), by simply changing poles" (p. 42).

17. Cone, *God of the Oppressed*, p. 16.

18. See James H. Cone, *The Spirituals and the Blues* (New York: Seabury, 1972).

19. See discussions on the black experience in Cone's *A Black Theology of Liberation*, pp. 54–57 and his *God of the Oppressed*, pp. 16–28. I have more to say on the problems with experience-driven biblical interpretation and theological reflection in chapter 3.

20. Cone, *God of the Oppressed*, p. 145. Cone makes these statements in the context of the occasional apocalyptic nature of some black preachers' messages.

21. Ibid., p. 23.

22. See a brief survey of this aspect of black church life in E. Franklin Frazier with C. Eric Lincoln, *The Negro Church in America/The Black Church Since Frazier* (New York: Schocken, 1974), pp. 35–51.

23. Gayraud S. Wilmore, *Black Religion and Black Radicalism: An Interpretation of the Religious History of Afro-American People* (Maryknoll, N.Y.: Orbis, 1984), p. 80.

24. Lester B. Scherer, *Slavery and the Churches in Early America: 1619–1819* (Grand Rapids: Eerdmans, 1975), p. 146.

25. Wilmore, *Black Religion and Black Radicalism*, pp. 80–81. Wilmore speaks of other church denominations that emerged after this event (pp. 84–98). Cone also refers

to the event of Allen and Jones leaving the St. George's church in *God of the Oppressed*, pp. 29, 141.

26. Wilmore, *Black Religion and Black Radicalism*, p. 36.

27. See Wilmore's treatment of these men in *Black Religion and Black Radicalism*, pp. 36–44.

28. Ibid., pp. 53–73.

29. See Wilmore's account in *Black Religion and Black Radicalism*, pp. 53–57. Lerone Bennett Jr. also reports the story in *Before the Mayflower: A History of Black America* (New York: Penguin, 1982), pp. 125–26.

30. Wilmore, *Black Religion and Black Radicalism*, p. 59. See Bennett's treatment of L'Ouverture in *Before the Mayflower*, pp. 117–25.

31. Wilmore, *Black Religion and Black Radicalism*, p. 61.

32. Ibid., p. 62.

33. Wilmore argues it is very unfortunate that many people today are familiar with Nat Turner through the fictionalized recreation of his life by William Styron, *The Confessions of Nat Turner* (New York: Random House, 1967). Though the book received the Pulitzer Prize during the late 1960s, it took great liberties with the life of Nat Turner. Wilmore further suggests that many readers of the book believed Styron had uncovered the network of black militancy's true motivations. These included black militancy's "paradoxical love-hate syndrome, its lust for power, and its futility—that others lacked the courage to disclose" (*Black Religion and Black Radicalism*, p. 63). Wilmore calls for a more evenhanded investigation of the historical data.

34. Ibid., p. 65. See an informative survey of Turner's rebellion in Bennett's *Before the Mayflower*, pp. 131–39.

35. Bennett, *Before the Mayflower*, p. 163.

36. Delores S. Williams, "Womanist Theology: Black Women's Voices," in *Black Theology*, vol. 2, p. 267. Williams sees Tubman as the kind of model for women's involvement in the liberation tradition that will inspire African-American "womanist" thinkers toward more needed reflection and action. Similar models may be hidden or de-emphasized in African-American history. "Womanist theology" is essentially doing theology from the perspective of African-American women in the United States by attempting a theological response to racism and sexism as uniquely experienced by African-American women.

37. Bennett, *Before the Mayflower*, p. 163.

38. Ibid., p. 166.

39. Bennett cites the thinking of abolitionist John Brown, who spoke of "talking" and "walking" abolitionists. Given this paradigm, Bennett holds that Sojourner Truth was a "talking" abolitionist and Harriet Tubman was a "walking" abolitionist (*Before the Mayflower*, pp. 163, 166).

40. Ibid., p. 163.

41. Cone, *Black Theology of Liberation*, pp. 63–64.

42. Ibid., p. 64. Deotis Roberts has expressed concern with Cone's "exclusive" Christology. He argues that Cone's christocentrism must be more inclusive or it will not be viable for the contextualization of black and African theologies. Roberts, however, does see latent christocentrism in both black and African theologies (J. Deotis Roberts, *Black Theology in Dialogue* [Philadelphia: Westminster, 1987], p. 41).

43. Cone, *Black Theology of Liberation*, p. 65.

44. Ibid., pp. 65–66. Cone's understanding of revelation is similar to Avery Dulles's category of revelation as "dialectical presence." For Cone one encounters God (or Jesus) in the midst of the struggle for liberation. For as assessment of this model of revelation, see Avery Dulles, *Models of Revelation* (Maryknoll, N.Y.: Orbis, 1994), pp. 93–97.

45. Cone, *Black Theology of Liberation*, p. 66.

46. Ibid., p. 67.

47. Cain Hope Felder, *Troubling Biblical Waters* (Maryknoll, N.Y.: Orbis, 1990), p. 14.

48. Cone, *God of the Oppressed*, p. 30.

49. Cited in ibid., p. 31.

50. Ibid., p. 33.

51. Ibid. Cone elucidates the force of this union between Christ the Liberator and the Church: "Can the Church of Jesus Christ be racist and Christian at the same time? Can the Church of Jesus Christ be politically, socially, and economically identified with the structures of oppression and also be a servant of Christ? Can the Church of Jesus Christ fail to make the liberation of the poor the center of its message and work, and still remain faithful to its Lord?" (p. 34).

52. Cone, *Black Theology of Liberation*, p. 68

53. Roberts, *Black Theology in Dialogue*, pp. 15–16.

54. Roberts argues that some theological perspectives have shown tendencies toward an "intellectual and spiritual neo-colonialism" (*Black Theology in Dialogue*, p. 15). The development of a liberative theology must be interdisciplinary in nature. It is only in dialogue with other philosophical and theological systems that such a liberation (black) theology can emerge. Theological systems that historically have not enjoyed a position of domination must be considered.

55. Cornel West identifies a number of factors that not only facilitated the emergence of the assumption of white supremacy in the West, but also explained both its pervasive nature in Western sociocultural settings and the perpetuation of such an assumption. Thus there are a number of "texts" of the historical, sociological, and economic sort that require exegesis (*Prophesy Deliverance* [Philadelphia: Westminster, 1982], pp. 48–49). Cain Hope Felder sees West's argument as providing legitimacy for skepticism on the part of black biblical scholars of the Western appropriation of the Scriptures (*Troubling Biblical Waters*, p. 8).

56. James H. Evans Jr., *We Have Been Believers: An African-American Systematic Theology* (Minneapolis: Fortress, 1992), p. 23.

57. Ibid., p. 15.

58. Ibid., p. 16. Evans suggests a pervasive interpretation that the exodus and the death and resurrection of Jesus are the foundations of Christian liberative hope in black theology.

59. See Evans's fuller discussion in *We Have Been Believers*, pp. 16–18.

60. Ibid., p. 23. Epistemology is the study of the origin, nature, and limits of knowledge. It considers the question, "How do we know what we know?" Evans asserts that black and white Christians see elements of the world differently. They come to know some things through diverse pathways of thought conditioned by their experiences. This diversity of perspective must be recognized and respected.

61. Ibid., pp. 23–24.

62. James H. Cone, "Christian Theology and Scripture as the Expression of God's Liberating Activity for the Poor," in *Speaking the Truth: Ecumenism, Liberation, and Black Theology* (Grand Rapids: Eerdmans, 1986), p. 5.

63. Ibid., pp. 5–6. This echoes a *christus victor* interpretation of the person and work of Christ. See Gustav Aulen, *Christus Victor* (London: SPCK, 1931).

64. Deotis Roberts has expressed some concern with Cone's christological focus. He suggests that such an emphasis may hinder dialogue with other theological perspectives as presented in the African context (*Black Theology in Dialogue*, p. 41). Roberts observes that Juan Luis Segundo lauds Cone's hermeneutical theory as one that successfully completes the hermeneutical circle through the experience of racism (J. Deotis Roberts, *Black Theology Today: Liberation and Contextualization* [New York: Mellen, 1983], p. 3). The hermeneutical circle begins with experience. In the realm of black theology, the experience of racism arouses an ideological suspicion, which extends to a questioning of all institutional structures, including theology. With the questioning of theology there arises a question of how Scripture has been read. This biblical hermeneutical suspicion leads to a new reading of Scripture. The circle is closed when this new reading of Scripture leads to further aid in the analysis of the present situation of oppression. See Roberts's criticism of Segundo in *Black Theology Today*, p. 7, and his criticism of both Segundo and Cone in *Black Theology in Dialogue*, p. 47.

65. Cone, *God of the Oppressed*, p. 102.

66. Roberts, *Black Theology Today*, p. 8.

67. Ibid., p. 9.

68. Ibid., p. 27.

69. Ibid., p. 28. Roberts shows concern here for two things. He wants to avoid "totalization," the idea that what should be considered universal is whatever those from an advantaged position choose for it to be. He is then careful to allow for the contextualization of theology in each and every culture.

70. Ibid.

71. Ibid., pp. 28–29.

72. J. Deotis Roberts, *The Prophethood of Black Believers: An African American Political Theology for Ministry* (Louisville: Westminster John Knox, 1994), p. 3.

73. Felder, *Troubling Biblical Waters*, p. 106.

74. Ibid., p. 114.

75. Stephen B. Reid, *Experience and Tradition: A Primer in Black Biblical Hermeneutics* (Nashville: Abingdon, 1990), p. 16.

76. Ibid., p. 19.

77. Ibid., p. 140.

78. Ibid., p. 141.

79. Ibid., p. 23. Reid labels these two elements as the *Imitatio Christi* and the *Christus Victor*, respectively.

80. Ibid., p. 25.

81. See Reid's subsequent readings of Genesis 3–4 (pp. 37–43) and Genesis 32 (pp. 45–47) following his argument that unity is based upon a particular understanding of God and of creation theology (pp. 26–33).

82. Ibid., p. 54.

83. Ibid., pp. 54–55.

84. Ibid., p. 85.

85. See the story Reid borrows from Henry Mitchell (*Black Preaching* [New York: Harper & Row, 1979]) to illustrate how critical awareness limited the extent of the recognized canon for black slaves (*Experience and Tradition*, p. 87).

86. Reid, *Experience and Tradition*, p. 29. See Reid's treatment of the meaning of the passage on pages 29–33.

87. Ibid., p. 142.

88. Rebecca S. Chopp and Mark Lewis Taylor, "Introduction: Crisis, Hope, and Contemporary Theology," in *Reconstructing Christian Theology*, ed. Rebecca S. Chopp and Mark Lewis Taylor (Minneapolis: Fortress, 1994), p. 4.

89. Cone, *God of the Oppressed*, p. 8.

90. Ibid.

91. Ibid. Cone's italics.

92. I will have more to say on this point in chapter 3.

Chapter 2: What Can Black Theology Teach the Evangelical Church?

1. This is to say that my black Baptist church background is not dramatically different from my present theological view of the church. In my system of thought, theology inherently includes the areas of function, mission, and the like.

2. Avery Dulles, *Models of the Church* (New York and London: Image Books, 1987).

3. Ibid., pp. 24–25.

4. Ibid., p. 37.

5. Dulles defines this authority: "The Church is not conceived as a democratic or representative society, but as one in which the fullness of power is concentrated in the hands of a ruling class that perpetuates itself by cooption" (*Models of the Church*, p. 38).

6. Charles H. Cooley, *Social Organization* (1909; reprint, New York: Schocken, 1967), pp. 23–31. Cited in Dulles, *Models of the Church*, p. 47.

7. Dulles, *Models of the Church*, p. 50.

8. Dulles argues that the image of the people of God is different from that of the body of Christ "in that it allows for a greater distance between the Church and its divine head" (ibid., p. 53). This facilitates the emergence of some themes favored by Protestant theology. These include the ideas of having a community where each person is individually free and of the church being in constant need of repentance and reform because it is both holy and sinful.

9. Ibid., p. 67. Dulles sees a sacrament as a sign of grace and as an efficacious sign. He argues that there is a distinction between a sign and a sacrament in its technical sense. "A sign could be a mere pointer to something that is absent, but a sacrament is a 'full sign,' a sign of something really present" (p. 66). As an efficacious sign, a sacrament produces that of which it is a sign. Though Dulles's distinction is helpful in understanding the nature of a sacrament, the comparison with a sign must be more carefully nuanced in light of biblical data. On the nature of *semeion* (sign) in the gospel of John, Otfried Hofius writes: "The Gospel itself stresses the historical reality of the events. At the same time the miracles are understood as signs pointing beyond themselves to the One who performs them" ("*Semeion*," in *New International Dictionary of the New Testament*, vol. 2, ed. Colin Brown [Grand Rapids: Zondervan, 1979], p. 632).

10. Dulles, *Models of the Church*, pp. 68–69. Dulles further argues that a link between the contemporary church and the church of apostolic times must be evident, "otherwise the Church could not appear as the sign of our redemption in and through the historical Christ" (p. 69).

11. Ibid., p. 76.

12. Ibid., p. 77. Dulles sees Karl Barth as a proponent of this type of ecclesiology.

13. "Since Vatican II the Servant Model has become popular because it satisfies a certain hunger for involvement in the making of a better world—a hunger that, although specifically Christian in motivation, establishes solidarity between the Church and the whole human family" (Dulles, *Models of the Church*, p. 31).

14. This interpretation of the mission of church comes from "The Pastoral Constitution on the Church in the Modern World," a part of the documents of Vatican II (Dulles, *Models of the Church*, p. 91).

15. I. Howard Marshall sees a correspondence between Jesus and the Son of Man when he writes that Jesus "speaks of the mission of the Son of Man as being to serve others and to give his life as a ransom for many, and he speaks of himself as the Son of man in reference to his impending betrayal and arrest (Mark 8:31, 9:9, 12, 31, 10:33, 45, 14:21a, b, 41)" ("Son of Man," in *Dictionary of Jesus and the Gospels*, ed. Scot McKnight et al. [Downers Grove, Ill.: InterVarsity, 1992], p. 776).

16. Dulles, *Models of the Church*, p. 173.

17. Ibid., p. 40. See his responses to each question as he discusses each model on the following pages: church as institution, pp. 40–41; as mystical communion, pp. 57–58; as sacrament, pp. 72–73; as herald, pp. 83–84; as servant, pp. 97–98.

18. These assessments are found on the following pages of Dulles, *Models of the Church*: Church as institution, pp. 42–45; as mystical union, pp. 58–61; as sacrament, pp. 73–75; as herald, pp. 84–88; as servant, pp. 98–102.

19. Some may label such a conservative perspective as *fundamentalist,* with all the negative connotations that this may carry. I identify this tradition as *evangelical,* a term I will develop more below.

20. See Alister McGrath's helpful summary on evangelicalism in his *Christian Theology: An Introduction* (Oxford: Blackwell, 1994), pp. 110–13. Carl F. H. Henry, considered by some to be the dean of modern evangelicalism, offers some observations on the identity of evangelicals. See his essay "Who Are the Evangelicals?" in *Evangelical Affirmations*, ed. Kenneth S. Kantzer and Carl F. H. Henry (Grand Rapids: Zondervan, 1990), pp. 69–94.

21. Alister E. McGrath, *Evangelicalism and the Future of Christianity* (Downers Grove, Ill.: InterVarsity, 1995), p. 55. A significant amount of discussion contained in this chapter is an incorporation of and response to this thought-provoking book.

22. Ibid., p. 59.

23. Ibid., p. 61.

24. McGrath states this point succinctly when he writes, "The only way Christianity can free itself from subservience to cultural fashion is to ensure that it is firmly grounded in a resource that is independent of that culture" (*Evangelicalism*, p. 63).

25. See a delineation of the implications of this transcendent view in C. S. Lewis, *Mere Christianity* (New York: Macmillan, 1972), pp. 55–56.

26. McGrath, *Evangelicalism*, p. 66.

27. Ibid., p. 67.

28. Ibid., p. 68.

29. Ibid. McGrath also discusses some background on charismatic movements, a discussion that extends into some comments on the contemporary scene as well (pp. 69–71).

30. McGrath refers to this as balancing concerns between members of a Word-based theology and members of a Spirit-based theology (ibid., p. 72). In addition, see Craig S. Keener, *Gift and Giver: The Holy Spirit in the Church Today* (Grand Rapids: Baker, 2001).

31. McGrath, *Evangelicalism*, p. 72.

32. Wayne Grudem, *Systematic Theology: An Introduction to Biblical Doctrine* (Grand Rapids: Zondervan, 1994), p. 709.

33. McGrath argues that this emphasis on evangelism comes from four considerations: "First, the need for a personal faith leads to the question of how that personal faith arises and the responsibility of believers toward that development. Second, the evangelical proclamation of the majesty of Christ as Savior and Lord naturally expresses itself in a concern to extend his kingdom. Third, the concern to remain faithful to Scripture means that the great biblical injunctions to proclaim Christ to the world (such as Matt. 28:18–20 and Acts 1:8) are taken with the utmost seriousness. And fourth, the intense joy of knowing Christ makes it natural for evangelicals to wish to share this experience with those whom they love, as an act of generosity and consideration" (*Evangelicalism*, pp. 75–76).

34. Ibid., pp. 78–79.

35. Robert J. Schreiter, *Constructing Local Theologies* (Maryknoll, N.Y.: Orbis, 1993), p. 4.

36. Schreiter holds that the gospel is more than just proclamation. It involves the practices of the community announcing the gospel along with an awareness of how the Word is already working among people in a missionary situation. It refers to the presence of the living Lord confronting the surrounding culture and sometimes confronting his own people. The church is a community existing in a particular sociocultural setting. It is also the connective to the teachings and practices of the past. Culture "represents a way of life for a given time and place, replete with values, symbols, and meanings, reaching out with hopes and dreams, often struggling for a better world" (*Constructing Local Theologies*, pp. 20–21).

37. See the treatment of pluralism and postmodernism in D. A. Carson, *The Gagging of God: Christianity Confronts Pluralism* (Grand Rapids: Zondervan, 1996), pp. 13–54.

38. David S. Cunningham, *Faithful Persuasion: In Aid of a Rhetoric of Christian Theology* (Notre Dame, Ind.: University of Notre Dame Press, 1991), p. xv. Elsewhere, Cunningham makes plain his thesis when he states that "the goal of Christian theology, then, is *faithful persuasion*: to speak the word that theology must speak, in ways that are faithful to the God of Jesus Christ and persuasive to the world that God has always loved" (p. 5, Cunningham's emphasis).

39. This is part of the reason Donald Bloesch writes in response to the possibility of ethics derived from "natural law": "Christian ethics cannot be grounded in natural law theory but instead must be rooted in the divine promise and the divine commandment as they are disclosed in the biblical revelation" (*A Theology of Word and Spirit* [Downers Grove, Ill.: InterVarsity, 1992], p. 169).

40. "The idea that faith and obedience belong together and cannot be separated is deeply embedded in the black church tradition" (James H. Cone, *For My People: Black Theology and the Black Church* [Maryknoll, N.Y.: Orbis, 1984], p. 154).

41. Tony Evans, *Let's Get to Know Each Other* (Nashville: Nelson, 1995), p. 66.

42. Patrick Bascio sees the interrelationship of theological categorization and ethical application in terms of the maintenance of the secular and the sacred in black theology: "It reflects its pragmatic roots in African religions, focusing on everyday concerns, in contrast with the Christian European obsession with personal salvation. By refusing to divide the world into secular and sacred, black theology nurtures and preaches a humanistic wholeness comfortable with a personal, familial God" (*The Failure of White Theology*, Martin Luther King Jr. Memorial Studies in Religion, Culture and Social Development, vol. 3 [New York: Lang, 1994], p. 4).

43. Cone, for example, advocates a view of the kingdom that invigorates believers to change present oppressive institutions as we move to the realm beyond: "A religion of liberation demands more than preaching, praying, and singing about the coming eschatological kingdom of God. It demands a critical theology based on the Bible and using the tools of the social sciences so that we can participate more effectively in establishing the kingdom in this world that we believe will be fully consummated in the next" (*For My People*, p. 120). James H. Evans Jr. places emphasis on the black eschatological vision of God's reign as overcoming bigotry, hatred and decimation of community in *We Have Been Believers* (Minneapolis: Fortress, 1992), p. 152.

44. Lester B. Scherer, *Slavery and the Churches in Early America, 1619–1819* (Grand Rapids: Eerdmans, 1975), p. 64.

45. Charles Hodge wrote such a defense in response to an earlier piece titled "Slavery" (1835) by William E. Channing, D.D., which attacked the institution of slavery (Channing's article is available at www3.edgenet.net/fcarpenter/slavery.html). The article by Hodge is in *Biblical Repertory and Princeton Review* 8 (1836): 268–304. His son, Alexander A. Hodge, summarized his father's priority in this matter and in all matters that require thought and response: "'What saith the Lord?' Nothing that the Bible pronounces true can be false; nothing is obligatory on the conscience but what it enjoins; nothing can be sin but what it condemns. If, therefore, the Scriptures under the Old Dispensation permitted men to hold slaves, and if the New Testament nowhere condemns slave-holding, but prescribes the relative duties of masters and slaves, then to pronounce slave-holding to be in itself sinful is contrary to Scripture" (*The Life of Charles Hodge* [New York: Arno Press and The New York Times, 1969], p. 334).

46. Philip H. Towner, "Household and Household Codes," in *Dictionary of Paul and His Letters*, ed. Gerald F. Hawthorne et al. (Downers Grove, Ill.: InterVarsity, 1993), p. 418.

47. Anthony C. Thiselton, "Truth (*aletheia*)," in *New International Dictionary of New Testament Theology*, vol. 3, ed. Colin Brown (Grand Rapids: Zondervan, 1979), p. 887.

48. Roger Nicole, "The Biblical Concept of Truth," in *Scripture and Truth*, ed. D. A. Carson and John D. Woodbridge (Grand Rapids: Zondervan, 1983), p. 293. He summarizes his study of the Old and New Testament on the meaning of *truth*: "The full Bible concept of truth involves factuality, faithfulness, and completeness" (p. 296).

49. Craig A. Evans, "Paul as Prophet," in *Dictionary of Paul and His Letters*, p. 764. Evans presents comparisons between Paul and the Old Testament prophets such as Jeremiah and Isaiah (pp. 762–65).

50. In June 1998, President Bill Clinton announced his intention to hold a committee on race relations in the U.S. Obviously, he and others saw a need for such dialogue even in the present day. Renowned pastor and Bible teacher Dr. Tony Evans recently wrote, "It would seem that after two hundred and fifty years, our country

would have long since addressed the problems of race and racism. Yet as we enter into the twenty-first century, this problem continues to plague us. It was in 1969 that I was told by the leadership of a large Southern Baptist church in Atlanta that I wasn't welcome there. It was in 1974 that my wife and I were informed in no uncertain terms that we were not welcome in a prominent Bible church in Dallas, pastored by the way, by one of my seminary professors. It was in 1987 that I was told by a number of major Christian radio station managers that there was little place for blacks in the general Christian broadcast media. And it was in 1993 that I heard a major influential national Christian leader say that, based on the curse of Ham, black people are under God's judgment" (*Let's Get to Know Each Other,* p. 117).

These examples are not mentioned to provide an extensive argument proving the persistent problem of racism. They are offered only to say, at this juncture, that the problem has not been eradicated, not even in the church of Jesus Christ.

51. What follows is a condensation of Millard Erickson's treatment in *Christian Theology* (Grand Rapids: Baker, 1991), pp. 627–31. For a survey of different views on the effect of sin in the life of men and women, see his survey on pp. 631–39.

52. Bloesch alerts us to the multifaceted nature of theological reflection when he writes, "Theology exists to serve the proclamation of the church. It will therefore be a kerygmatic theology, focusing on the message of faith. But it will also have a prophetic dimension, endeavoring to bring the law of God to bear upon both personal and social sin. Finally, it will have an apologetic dimension, for it will make a determined effort to unmask the powers of the world that challenge and attack the church. Yet in fulfilling its apologetic mandate it will not presume that arguments for the faith can ever induce faith in unbelievers, for faith comes only by the hearing of the Word of God (Rom. 10:17)" (*A Theology of Word and Spirit,* p. 128).

53. J. A. Thompson writes, "The *heart* of man (*leb*) in the psychology of OT times refers frequently to the mind, the source of a man's thinking and action. It is here described as *deceitful* above all" (*The Book of Jeremiah* [Grand Rapids: Eerdmans, 1981], pp. 421–22). Erickson includes this passage in the Old Testament foundations for the "intensiveness of sin" (*Christian Theology,* p. 625). Intensiveness is another way of describing pervasiveness.

54. Douglas Moo, *Romans 1–8* (Chicago: Moody, 1991), p. 341. Moo gives extensive attention to the treatment of this verse on pp. 328–41. Herman Ridderbos, however, sees Paul's pronouncement in Romans 5:12 as a basis for the shared penalty of death with Adam rather than as a basis for the sinful nature of the Adamic race (*Paul: An Outline of His Theology* [Grand Rapids: Eerdmans, 1982], pp. 98–107).

55. Erickson, *Christian Theology,* p. 638.

56. As I am proceeding through these reflections, I am not suggesting that white members of the church are the only ones who have a problem with racism. As we shall see later in this work, African-Americans can also have the disease. Because of our history and its present-day effects, however, racism among the white church community must be scrutinized intensely.

57. The Genesis narrative shows that some development occurs in Joseph's understanding of his imprisonment in the context of God's plan. He correctly claims that he has done nothing worthy of imprisonment (Gen. 40:15). After successfully interpreting Pharaoh's dreams (Gen. 41:16–36), he is rewarded. The event of naming his sons, Manasseh and Ephraim (Gen. 41:50–52), shows a growing understanding of what God was doing. Joseph clearly states his perspective of God's design in Gen. 50:20: "You intended

to harm me, but God intended it for good to accomplish what is now being done, the saving of many lives."

58. This interpretation is presented by Ernst Haenchen, *The Acts of the Apostles: A Commentary* (Philadelphia: Westminster, 1971), p. 281. F. F. Bruce presents a similar understanding: "Here again Stephen traces a pattern of Jewish behaviour which was to find its complete and final expression when Christ Himself appeared among them as the Saviour provided by God" (*The Book of the Acts* [Grand Rapids: Eerdmans, 1981], p. 150).

59. W. H. Grispen, *Exodus* (Grand Rapids: Eerdmans, 1982), p. 43. Brevard S. Childs also concludes that Moses required secrecy because he had no authority. He writes, "The impudent Hebrew saw this correctly" (*The Book of Exodus* [Philadelphia: Westminster, 1974], p. 31).

60. Bruce follows the same train of thought when in his closing comment on Acts 7:51 he writes, "Moses and the prophets had described the fathers in these terms; they are equally true, says Stephen, of their children of the contemporary generation" (*Acts*, p. 162).

61. George D. Kelsey, *Racism and the Christian Understanding of Man* (New York: Charles Scribner's Sons, 1965), p. 9.

62. Erickson argues that the doctrine of God is fundamental in the formulation of any theological system: "The doctrine of God is the central point for the rest of theology. One's view of God might even be thought of as supplying the whole framework within which one's theology is constructed and life is lived. It lends a particular coloration of one's style of ministry and philosophy of life" (*Christian Theology*, p. 263).

63. I will not engage in debate on a possible Deutero- or Trito-Isaiah. I am simply referring to it in its canonical form.

64. Other passages that inculcate a burden for a true and accurate picture of God through witness to his actions are Numbers 14:10–16, Jeremiah 23:15–18, and Ezekiel 36:22.

65. Kelsey, *Racism*, p. 27.

66. McKenzie defines etiology as "a story that is invented to explain the origin of something—a name, a place, a custom, or even a geological formation" (*All God's Children: A Biblical Critique of Racism* [Louisville: Westminster John Knox, 1997], pp. 6–7).

67. Ibid., p. 7.

68. Kelsey argues that racism, like any faith system, "is an expression of the will to believe" (*Racism*, p. 24).

69. Ibid., p. 27.

70. Ibid., p. 26, citing H. Richard Niebuhr's *Radical Monotheism and Western Culture* (New York: Harper, 1960), p. 16.

71. Kelsey, *Racism*, pp. 28–29, citing Ruth Benedict, *Race: Science and Politics* (New York: Viking, 1947), p. 98.

72. For an extended treatment on the nature and function of the image of God, see Philip Edgcumbe Hughes, *The True Image: Christ as the Origin and Destiny of Man* (Grand Rapids: Eerdmans, 1989), pp. 3–69.

73. Kelsey, *Racism*, p. 74.

74. Ibid., p. 27.

75. For some discussion on the appropriate terms to describe the influence of demons on human beings, see Sydney H. T. Page, *Powers of Evil: A Biblical Study of Satan and Demons* (Grand Rapids: Baker, 1995), pp. 137–38.

76. Graham H. Twelftree observes: "In harmony with beliefs of that day, the Gospels depict demons causing convulsion, loud screaming, a change of voice or character, chaotic and unpredictable behavior, preternatural strength and an indifference to pain. Notably, a disturbance is caused by and in the sufferer when confronted by Jesus (Mark 1:21–28, 5:1–20, 7:24–30, 9:14–29 and par.). Also, the demon possessed were considered to have special insight into the identity of Jesus (Mark 1:24, 3:11; cf. Acts 16:17)" ("Demon, Devil, Satan," in *Dictionary of Jesus and the Gospels*, ed. Scott McKnight et al. [Downers Grove, Ill.: InterVarsity, 1992], p. 165).

77. Kelsey has a rather insightful perspective on the nature of a harmful stereotype: "The stereotype is a device which is used to persuade, not to inform" (*Racism*, p. 43).

78. We do not wish to adopt the state of mind of the person whom Kelsey describes as one who "has overcome prejudice": "I simply say to myself, 'He is just like me, after all. He is cultivated, refined, and charming in spite of being a Negro. In short, I forget his being a Negro, and think of him culturally as being like me.' The narrator of such accounts, even though Christian, never realizes that he has annihilated the being whom God created and translated that being into his own image" (*Racism*, p. 67).

79. Francis A. Schaeffer, "The Mark of the Christian," in *The Church at the End of the 20th Century* (Downers Grove, Ill.: InterVarsity, 1970), p. 133. InterVarsity Press also published this chapter separately as a short pamphlet.

80. Ibid., p. 137.

81. Ibid., p. 139.

82. This idea could be derived from those who accentuate the political power dimension of racism. George C. L. Cummings is not one who specifically states that African-Americans cannot be racist because they lack social-political power. Instead, he emphasizes a political power confrontation with racism when he calls for a "political rhetoric of emancipation out of oppressive situations." He continues, "By treating them as rhetorical, I construe theologies as discourses of persuasion. By treating them as political I indicate my conviction that all discourses are construed out of, and create postures toward, the social order, even when they include no specific references to such matters" (George C. L. Cummings, "New Voices in Black Theology," in *Black Theology: A Documentary History, Volume Two: 1980–1992*, ed. James H. Cone and Gayraud S. Wilmore [Maryknoll, N.Y.: Orbis, 1993], p. 73).

83. Denise M. Ackerman, "Power," in *Dictionary of Feminist Theologies*, ed. Letty M. Russell and J. Shannon Clarkson (Louisville: Westminster John Knox, 1996), pp. 219–20.

84. I will address this issue more directly under my discussion of systemic sin. An example must suffice for the present. In "Racism: America's Original Sin," Dr. Loretta Williams cites what is assumed to be a repeated model: "You have a number of people who are saying, 'I did believe that with my Harvard degree and my Stanford MBA I would get to be CEO of a company, and now am understanding that I'm never going to be a CEO, I'm never going to be fast-tracked in the same way as my white colleagues'" (Interview, January/February 1994, available at http://sunsite.unc.edu/spc/articles/1.94.html).

85. I do not wish to sound extreme, but it is possible for many whites, including those in the church, to regard African-Americans as persons, though not in the same

way as they regard themselves as persons. Kelsey alluded to the possibility of such a view when he wrote of the assignment of statuses to African-Americans in America: "First, the Negro exists as an isolated and subordinated man. Second, in some contexts, he 'exists' as a nonentity" (*Racism*, p. 41).

86. See Kelsey's discussion in *Racism*, pp. 53–56.

87. I realize that I am treating Philippians 2:5–11 as paradigmatic, that is, with Christ as a model for believers. For an extended survey of other views, see Ralph P. Martin, *Carmen Christi: Philippians 2:5–11 in Recent Interpretation and in the Setting of Early Christian Worship* (Grand Rapids: Eerdmans, 1983). In recent days some have challenged the view of the atonement that presents suffering as redemptive and positive. I will discuss this in chapter 3.

88. Kelsey, *Racism*, pp. 58–59. The last sentence is from Martin Buber, *I and Thou*, trans. Ronald Gregor Smith (Edinburgh: Clark, 1937), p. 11.

89. Feminist theologians are also among those giving attention to this pervasive element of the doctrine of sin. For example, Marjorie Hewitt Suchocki writes, "Feminists have given sustained attention to the social and cultural factors of oppression and foster sins of victims. Rather than confining sin to the personal sphere, feminists look to social structures and their effects on the human psyche and on human behavior" ("Sin," in *Dictionary of Feminist Theologies*, p. 262).

90. Emilio Nuñez correctly observes about Metz: "He notes that the Bible uses political categories in referring to God: kingdom, lordship, power. Furthermore, the God of the Bible promotes liberating movements. The kingdom of God means the integral liberation of the poor as persons, not only as souls" (Emilio Antonio Nuñez, *Liberation Theology*, trans. Paul E. Sywulka [Chicago: Moody, 1985], pp. 44–45).

91. For a detailed treatment on various millennial views, see Stanley J. Grenz, *The Millennial Maze* (Downers Grove, Ill.: InterVarsity, 1992).

92. Erickson, *Christian Theology*, pp. 641–58.

93. Ibid., p. 655.

94. Ibid. p. 658.

Chapter 3: What Is the Future of Black Theology?

1. J. Deotis Roberts, *Black Theology in Dialogue* (Philadelphia: Westminster, 1987), p. 7.

2. "The time is different. They feel a different kind of intellectual energy and spiritual urgency. They are not trying to justify their right to do theology. They assume it, with no apology to Whites" (*Black Theology: A Documentary History, Volume Two: 1980–1992*, ed. James H. Cone and Gayraud S. Wilmore [Maryknoll, N.Y.: Orbis, 1993], pp. 4–5).

3. James H. Cone, *For My People: Black Theology and the Black Church* (Maryknoll, N.Y.: Orbis, 1984) pp. 86–98.

4. Ibid., p. 88.

5. Ibid., p. 97.

6. Ronald C. Potter, "The New Black Evangelicals," in *Black Theology: A Documentary History, Volume One: 1966–1979*, ed. James H. Cone and Gayraud S. Wilmore (Maryknoll, N.Y.: Orbis, 1979), p. 307.

7. William H. Bentley, "Origins and Focus of the N.B.E.A.," in *Black Theology*, vol. 1, p. 318.

8. For the purpose of comparing the thought of various black theologians on the issue of theodicy and defending the character of God in the face of the presence and manifestations of evil, Anthony Pinn uses John Hick's categories (John Hick, *Philosophy of Religion*, 4th ed. [Englewood Cliffs, N.J.: Prentice Hall, 1990]): "The resolution of the problem of evil can take various forms: (1) a rethinking of the nature/purpose of evil; or, (2) the postulating of a 'limited' God; or, (3) a questioning/denial of God's existence. Although Hick does not address it, there is a fourth possible resolution that entails questioning God's goodness and/or righteousness" (Anthony B. Pinn, *Why Lord? Suffering and Evil in Black Theology* [New York: Continuum, 1995], p. 14).

9. Pinn, *Why Lord?*, p. 11. Luther's statement at the Diet of Worms is as follows: "My conscience is captive to the Word of God. Thus I cannot and will not recant, for going against my conscience is neither safe nor salutary. I can do no other, here I stand, God help me. Amen" (Cited in Heiko A. Oberman, *Luther: Man Between God and the Devil* [New York and London: Doubleday/Image, 1992], p. 203).

10. I am not suggesting that an appeal merely to the conscience of the United States, or to any oppressive country for that matter, is sufficient in and of itself. Some ideological and theological common ground must be established if there is to be any hope for a reconciliation that respects diversity while recognizing the need for unity.

11. On the matter of rage, the poor in the inner cities are not the only ones who have to cope with this. Garth Kasimu Baker-Fletcher, an associate professor of ethics at the Claremont School of Theology, relates his irritation with some colleagues and students who attempted to address him with language reflective of an inaccurate understanding of black English: "The irritation came from the fact that these were students and staff who knew me, had read my resume, knew that I held advanced degrees from Harvard and had penned several articles. None of those things made any difference to them. They saw, I believed, an 'uppity nigger' who needed to be brought down a few pegs, and they were glad to do it" (*Xodus: An African American Male Journey* [Minneapolis: Fortress, 1996], p. 160).

12. There are, admittedly, differences in view on the nature and function of the black church. Gayraud S. Wilmore sees the black church in the midst of an identity crisis: "The Black Church, in other words, is still in the throes of a crisis of identity and the primary emphasis of Black Theology, viz., that the Black Christian struggle for liberation unconceals (Herzog) the essence of the gospel and is therefore confirmed by it, lies on the other side of the crisis which most Black Christians today find to be a slow and painful transition" (Wilmore, "Introduction: Part IV—Black Theology and the Black Church," in *Black Theology*, vol. 1, p. 244). Though I have great sympathy with Wilmore's call for an expanded understanding of liberation, I remain unconvinced that the achievement of liberation can be accomplished only with a wholesale redefinition of what constitutes the church and its mission.

13. Joseph H. Jackson, "The Basic Theological Position of the National Baptist Convention, U.S.A., Inc." in *Black Theology*, vol. 1, p. 259.

14. Wilmore holds that this Negro Church "lives on, but is always in transition to a more authentic expression of its historic identity and, therefore, its ineluctable vocation in American society" (Wilmore, "Introduction: Part IV," p. 247).

15. Ibid., p. 246.

16. James H. Cone, "Black Theology and the Black Church: Where Do We Go from Here?" in *Black Theology*, vol. 1, p. 354.

17. James H. Evans Jr., *We Have Been Believers* (Minneapolis: Fortress, 1992), p. 134.

18. Ibid., p. 135.

19. Ibid., pp. 135–36. Evans does not present a fully developed doctrine of the Holy Spirit, but he does show an awareness of trinitarian distinctives (particularly p. 135).

20. Ibid., p. 137.

21. Dennis W. Wiley, "Black Theology, the Black Church, and the African-American Community," in *Black Theology*, vol. 2, p. 132.

22. I would admit without any hesitation that belief statements can be misused. For example, see an exploration of the relationship between certain eschatological views with the views of white supremacy in James H. Evans Jr., "Eschatology, White Supremacy and the Beloved Community," in *Reconstructing Christian Theology*, ed. Rebecca S. Chopp and Mark Lewis Taylor (Minneapolis: Fortress, 1994), pp. 346–73.

23. For a treatment on the interrelationship of exegetical, biblical, and historical theologies as they relate to the derivation of systematic theology, see D. A. Carson, "Unity and Diversity in the New Testament: The Possibility of Systematic Theology," in *Scripture and Truth*, ed. D. A. Carson and John D. Woodbridge (Grand Rapids: Baker, 1998), pp. 90–93. See also Grant R. Osborne, *The Hermeneutical Spiral* (Downers Grove, Ill.: InterVarsity, 1991), pp. 286–317.

24. Anthony C. Thiselton, *New Horizons in Hermeneutics* (Grand Rapids: Zondervan, 1992), p. 410.

25. Ibid., p. 379. Thiselton's italics.

26. Ibid., p. 410. Thiselton's italics.

27. James H. Cone, *A Black Theology of Liberation* (Philadelphia: Lippincott, 1970), p. 76. In an earlier monumental work, Cone called attention to the relationship between problems in the sociocultural setting in the United States and problems in theology: "For the sickness of the Church in America is intimately involved with the bankruptcy of American theology. When the Church fails to live up to its appointed mission, it means that theology is partly responsible. Therefore, it is impossible to criticize the Church and its lack of relevancy without criticizing theology for its failure to perform its function" (*Black Theology and Black Power* [New York: Seabury, 1969], p. 83).

28. James H. Evans Jr., "Toward an African-American Theology," in *Black Theology*, vol. 2, p. 32.

29. George C. L. Cummings, "New Voices in Black Theology: The African-American Story as a Source of Emancipatory Rhetoric," in *Black Theology*, vol. 2, p. 71.

30. There is disagreement on the part of some concerning the proportion of African influence on the black church. E. Franklin Frazier, for example, suggests an African influence severely diminished by the impact of the enslavement process: "In studying any phase of the character and the development of the social and cultural life of the Negro in the United States, one must recognize from the beginning that because of the manner in which the Negroes were captured in Africa and enslaved, they were practically stripped of their social heritage" (E. Franklin Frazier with C. Eric Lincoln, *The Negro Church in America/The Black Church Since Frazier* [New York: Schocken, 1974], p. 9). Dwight N. Hopkins, however, writes: "One has to acknowledge the convergence of a reinterpreted white Christianity with the remains of African religions under slavery. It was precisely in the 'Invisible Institution' that slavery synthesized these two foundational God-encounters to form slave theology" ("Slave Theology in the Invisible Institution," in *Cut Loose Your Stammering Tongue*, ed. Dwight N. Hopkins and

George C. L. Cummings [Maryknoll, N.Y.: Orbis, 1992], p. 4). The "Invisible Institution" was a name given to the practice of the secret worship of God by the slaves when this type of gathering was forbidden by the slave holders.

31. George C. L. Cummings, "Slave Narratives, Black Theology of Liberation (USA), and the Future," in *Cut Loose Your Stammering Tongue*, p. 141.

32. "The genius of the African American slave experience is that it rejects a theological dialogue about the theodicy question; it acknowledges evil as a reality; and through imaginative mythopoetic and linguistic identification with Jesus the Crucified One combined with the traditional African world-view, it came to view the black slave community as the recipient of God's gracious Spirit, who would ensure ultimate liberation" (ibid., p. 146).

33. "A Panel Discussion: Lindbeck, Hunsinger, McGrath and Fackre," in *The Nature of Confession: Evangelicals and Postliberals in Conversation*, ed. Timothy R. Phillips and Dennis L. Okholm (Downers Grove, Ill.: InterVarsity, 1996), p. 251. McGrath is responding to members of the postliberal movement, those who hold to many of the confessions of orthodox Christianity but see these confessions as authoritative and relevant exclusively to the church. They raise serious objections to the universal application of these confessions to people and thought systems outside of the church community. Many black theologians, through various means, will accomplish essentially the same thing. Their system of confession will equip them to speak only to the liberation community and render them ineffective in persuading others to their view.

34. James H. Cone, *God of the Oppressed* (Maryknoll, N.Y.: Orbis, 1997), p. 8 (Cone's emphasis).

35. Cone, *Black Theology of Liberation*, p. 18. William H. Bentley points out that not all in the black theological community hold the exodus event as the most helpful model of Divine involvement in the liberation struggle ("Origins and Focus of the N.B.E.A.," p. 315).

36. I realize that in the name of a more critical approach to the Old Testament, I should have used the designation of Trito-Isaiah. I am reading, however, in a canonical manner, much in the way that I was taught in my African-American Baptist heritage.

37. The New Testament uses such Old Testament titles to refer to the church (e.g., 1 Pet. 2:9). The debate on the nature of continuity and discontinuity between the Old Testament and the New Testament is a discussion well beyond the scope of the present work. Suffice it to say that I am pursuing a point of continuity, namely, that God demands obedience from his own as the only appropriate response to the covenant relationship he institutes with his people.

38. Peter C. Craigie, *The Book of Deuteronomy* (Grand Rapids: Eerdmans, 1976), p. 187.

39. This is the force of Philippians 2:13: "For it is God who works in you to will and to act according to his good purpose." Augustine expressed a related idea in the *Confessions* 10.29: "Give what you command, and then command whatever you will."

40. Robert Letham defines the work of Christ as "all that Christ did when he came to this earth 'for us and our salvation,' all that he continues to do now that he is risen from the dead and at God's right hand, and all that he will do when he returns in glory at the end of the age" (*The Work of Christ* [Downers Grove, Ill.: InterVarsity, 1993], pp. 18–19).

41. Along with Letham's work in *The Work of Christ* (pp. 159–75), see Bruce Demarest, *The Cross and Salvation* (Wheaton, Ill.: Crossway, 1997), pp. 149–66. For a biblical and theological treatment of the atonement, see Leon Morris, *The Atonement: Its Meaning and Significance* (Downers Grove, Ill.: InterVarsity, 1983).

42. See a brief discussion on the matter in Donald Bloesch, *Jesus Christ: Savior and Lord* (Downers Grove, Ill.: InterVarsity, 1997), pp. 167–70.

43. I realize that womanist theology has some unique characteristics of its own, but I incorporate it here under the topic of black theology because it does share much in terms of burdens with this movement.

44. Cone, *God of the Oppressed*, p. 160.

45. Ibid., p. 161.

46. J. Christaan Beker sees in Christ's cross "the eschatological judgment of the apocalyptic powers. 'The rulers of this age' have 'crucified the Lord of glory' (1 Cor. 2:8); the rebellion of the world and its powers against God reaches its climax in the death of Christ. But it is precisely in the cross of Christ that the world itself is judged" (*The Triumph of God: The Essence of Paul's Thought* [Minneapolis: Fortress, 1990], pp. 81–82). Beker correctly sees the cross of Christ as the effectual overpowering of all temporal powers, physical and spiritual, and as the guarantee of God's sole eternal rule.

47. Surrogacy is associated with black women being substituted into other people's roles and functions. Williams further explains the distinction of involuntary and voluntary surrogacy, a comparison of times under slavery and emancipation: "For example, black female slaves were forced to substitute for the slave-owner's wife in nurturing roles involving white children. Black women were forced to take the place of men in work roles that, according to the larger society's understanding of male and female roles, belonged to men. . . . The difference was that black women after emancipation could exercise the choice of refusing the surrogate role, but social pressures often influenced the choices black women made as they adjusted to life in a free world" (Delores S. Williams, *Sisters in the Wilderness* [Maryknoll, N.Y.: Orbis, 1993], pp. 60–61). The pervasive problems of racism, sexism, and classism contribute to the social setting that perpetuates surrogacy for black females.

48. Sympathetic assessments of Williams's thought can be found in JoAnne Marie Terrell, *Power in the Blood: The Cross in the African American Experience* (Marynoll, N.Y.: Orbis, 1998), pp. 99–125, and in Mark L. Chapman, *Christianity on Trial: African-American Religious Thought Before and After Black Power* (Maryknoll, N.Y.: Orbis, 1996), pp. 159–62.

49. Williams, *Sisters in the Wilderness*, p. 167.

50. Ibid., p. 164. Williams's italics.

51. Ibid., p. 165.

52. Ibid., pp. 162–64.

53. Demarest, *Cross and Salvation*, p. 167. He shows numerous passages throughout the New Testament that speak of the cross as well as the suffering and death of Christ.

54. I concede the fact that through the artistry of a discipline such as form-criticism, this passage and others like it could be rendered totally irrelevant for commentary on this matter. I am of the opinion that it is a part of the canonical text, a view long held and long believed in the church. For a discussion on the authenticity of this passage see D. A. Carson, *The Expositor's Bible Commentary with the New International Version: Matthew (Chapters 13–28)* (Grand Rapids: Zondervan, 1995), pp. 432–33.

55. Other passages adjoin the mission of Jesus to the force of his death. See, for example, references from John's Gospel: Jesus as the "Lamb of God" (John 1:29, 36); and Jesus' indication of coming for the purpose of dying (John 12:27; see also vv. 32–33).

56. Erickson, *Christian Theology* (Grand Rapids: Baker, 1991), p. 811.

57. Ibid., p. 803.

58. See the full treatment in Letham, *Work of Christ*, pp. 125–57.

59. Ibid., p. 132.

60. Ibid., p. 138.

61. Herwart Vorlander and Colin Brown, "*katallasso*," in *New International Dictionary of New Testament Theology*, vol. 3, ed. Colin Brown (Grand Rapids: Zondervan, 1979), p. 167. I do not wish to ignore the interpersonal and intercommunity dimension of reconciliation (1 Cor. 7:11; Matt. 5:24), but this will receive concentrated attention in a future contribution to this series by Raleigh Washington.

62. Letham, *Work of Christ*, p. 144.

63. Ibid., pp. 149–50.

64. Erickson, *Christian Theology*, p. 473.

65. Letham, *Work of Christ*, p. 152.

66. For a fuller treatment on these matters, see Anthony A. Hoekema, *Created in God's Image* (Grand Rapids: Eerdmans, 1986).

67. Emil Brunner, "Man and Creation," in *Readings in Christian Theology*, vol. 2, ed. Millard J. Erickson (Grand Rapids: Baker, 1986), p. 47.

68. My concern in this particular issue is to address those in the black theological community who claim the title "Christian," who hold the Bible as the Word of God and therefore authoritative for faith and practice, and who then seek to build up the African-American community in all ways needed.

69. Dwight N. Hopkins and Linda E. Thomas, "Black Theology U.S.A. Revisited," *Journal of Theology for Southern Africa* 100 (1998): 63. This article offers a brief survey and summary of representatives in the womanist theological community. For a helpful exposure to womanist theological reflections on the problem of evil, see *A Troubling in My Soul: Womanist Perspectives on Evil and Suffering*, ed. Emilie M. Towns (Maryknoll, N.Y.: Orbis, 1993).

70. "Roundtable Discussion: Christian Ethics and Theology in Womanist Perspective," *Journal of Feminist Studies in Religion* 5 (1989): 83–112. This article also includes responses by various members of the womanist theological community.

71. Ibid., p. 87. Sanders offers the following delineation of Walker's definition as it may be applied to black feminists: "The womanist is a black feminist who is audacious, willful and serious; loves and prefers women, but also may love men; is committed to the survival and wholeness of entire people, and is universalist, capable, all loving, and deep" (p. 86). See a fuller presentation of this definition in Williams, *Sisters in the Wilderness*, p. 243, n. 5.

72. "Christian Ethics," p. 90.

73. Though I do not agree with his train of thought, see Elias Farajaje-Jones, "Breaking Silence: Toward An In-The-Life Theology," in *Black Theology*, vol. 2, p. 141.

74. In one of his summary statements on Romans 1:18–32, Richard B. Hays concludes: "Homosexual acts are not, however, specially reprehensible sins; they are no worse than any of the other manifestations of human unrighteousness listed in the passage (vv. 29–31)—no worse in principle than covetousness or gossip or disrespect for

parents" (*The Moral Vision of the New Testament: A Contemporary Introduction to New Testament Ethics* [New York: HarperSanFrancisco, 1996], p. 388).

75. Ibid., p. 391.

76. In a section where he wrestles with the possibility of other authorities deserving to be consulted on the matter of homosexuality, Hays comments on the role of experience and its relationship to Scripture: "In any case, it is crucial to remember that experience must be treated as a hermeneutical lens for reading the New Testament rather than as an independent counterbalancing authority" (ibid., p. 399).

77. Ibid., p. 401.

78. Frederick Douglass, *Narrative of the Life of Frederick Douglass: An American Slave* (1845; reprint, New York: Penguin/Signet, 1997), p. 118.

79. Desmond Tutu, *Crying in the Wilderness* (Grand Rapids: Eerdmans, 1982), p. 114.

80. Robert J. Schreiter, *The Ministry of Reconciliation: Spirituality and Strategies* (Maryknoll, N.Y.: Orbis, 1998), p. 66. Schreiter's italics.

81. Ibid., p. 75

Subject Index

Subject Index

reform of 41
as sacrament 39, 40–41
as servant 39, 41
class 33, 124 n. 47
Clinton, Bill 116 n. 50
communication 35
community 29, 30, 34, 46, 63–64, 66,
    73, 76
Cone, James 13, 32–33, 75, 81, 82,
    86–88
  on black experience 15–16
  Christology of 90–91, 110 n. 42
  on revelation 21–23
  on Scripture 26–27
  on second generation of black
      theologians 71–72
  on task of black theologian 34–36
  on tradition 23–24
conquest, atonement as 93, 95
contextualization 111 n. 69
conversion 45
Cooley, Charles H. 39
Craigie, Peter 88
creation 40
critical awareness 33
criticism 71–72, 84
cross 44, 90–91
  See also atonement
cultural liberation 25
culture 47, 114 n. 36
Cummings, George C. L. 82, 83, 119
    n. 82
Cunningham, David 48

death 95
dehumanization 13, 26, 34, 35, 63,
    65–66, 79, 84, 87
Demarest, Bruce 92
demons 62, 96
depravity 53–56
Diet of Worms 74
discipleship 100–101
docetic theology 50
doctrine 77–78
dogmatic development 84
dogmatism 36
domination 80

Douglass, Frederick 103
Dulles, Avery 38–42, 110 n. 44

economic analysis 72
Edwards, Jonathan 51
empowerment 27
epistemology 25, 111 n. 60
Erickson, Millard 53–54, 68–69, 95,
    116 n. 51, 118 n. 62
ethics 49–50
ethnic groups 33
Eurocentric theologians 77–78
evangelicalism 42–46, 107 n. 1, 113
    n. 19
evangelism 44–45, 114 n. 33
Evans, James 24–25, 76, 82, 115 n. 43
Evans, Tony 50, 116 n. 50
exegesis 27, 35
exodus tradition 18, 31, 87–88
experience 16, 23, 73, 93

faith 60, 68
family 52, 74, 99
Felder, Cain Hope 22, 26, 32–33, 110
    n. 55
feminist theology 15, 34, 79, 80, 120
    n. 89
forgiveness 104–5
Frazier, E. Franklin 122 n. 30
freedom 14, 19, 31, 33, 87, 89
Freire, Paulo 14
fundamentalism 113 n. 19

gay and lesbian theologies 34
gender 33, 72
God 86–89
  identification with black people
      13–14, 21
  liberating activities 16
  power 27
  solidarity with oppressed 26, 27, 90
gospel 103, 114 n. 36
grace 40, 44, 102
Gray, Thomas R. 19
Grispen, W. H. 55
Grudem, Wayne 45

Haenchen, Ernst 117 n. 58
Haiti 18

Subject Index

pastoral theology 32
patriarchy 84
patriotism 30, 31, 32
penal substitution 93–94
personhood 14, 21, 100–101
persuasion 48–49
Philadelphia 17
philosophy 35–36
physical liberation 25
Pinn, Anthony 73–74
political theology 32
polytheism 60
postliberalism 123 n. 33
postmodernity 48
Potter, Ronald 73
power 64–66, 80
preaching 45
premillennialism 68
privatized faith 68
proclamation 41
prophets 35
Prosser, Gabriel 18, 20
provincialism 104

racism 13, 14, 15, 31, 43, 46, 50, 51, 52, 57, 72, 84, 96, 116 n. 50, 124 n. 47
  as faith and idolatry 57–67
  institutional 72
reconciliation 41, 93, 94–95, 104–5
Reid, Stephen B. 26, 29–33
repentance 41, 69
revelation 23, 110 n. 44
Richmond, Virginia 18
Ridderbos, Herman 117 n. 54
righteousness 28
Roberts, J. Deotis 13, 23, 24, 26, 27–28, 32–33, 71, 82, 110 n. 42, 111 n. 64
Roman Catholicism 39, 41, 42

sacrament 113 n. 9
salvation 26, 75, 101–2
Sanders, Cheryl 99
Satan 95
Schaeffer, Francis A. 63–64
Scherer, Lester 17
Schreiter, Robert 47, 104

Segundo, Juan Luis 111 n. 64
self-criticism 71–72
self-knowledge 25
sexism 72, 124 n. 47
sin 53, 67, 87, 101
slaveholding religion 103
slavery 18, 19–21, 50, 82–83
social manipulation 80
social sciences 72, 73
social sin 68
sociocultural dynamics 33–34, 80, 88–89, 92–93
spiritual empowerment 25
Stephen 55–56
Styron, William 109 n. 33
substitutionary atonement 91, 93
Suchocki, Marjorie Hewitt 120 n. 89
suffering 91
suffering/critical awareness 30, 31, 32
surrogacy 91–92, 124 n. 47
systemic sin 46, 63, 67–69

Taylor, Mark Lewis 34
teachers 35
theological training 43, 83
theology
  contextual nature of 46, 47–51
  as local 47–48
  melting pot model 34
  western domination of 23
Thiselton, Anthony 52, 79–80
Thompson, J. A. 117 n. 53
tradition 23–24
truth 52
Truth, Sojourner 20
Tubman, Harriet 20, 109 nn. 36, 39
Turner, Nat 18, 19, 20, 109 n. 33
Tutu, Desmond 103
Twelftree, Graham H. 118 n. 76

Underground Railroad 20
unity 30, 32, 39, 64

Vatican II 41, 113 n. 13
Vesey, Denmark 18–19, 20
Walker, Alice 99
Walker, David 18
West, Cornel 110 n. 55

130

Subject Index

white oppression 13, 14–15
white theology 50–51, 82
Wiley, Dennis 76, 75
Williams, Delores 91–93
Williams, Loretta 119 n. 84
Wilmore, Gayraud S. 17–18, 19, 75, 82, 121 n. 12

womanist theology 34, 90, 99, 109 n. 36, 125 n. 69
women, in black church 20–21, 92
works-righteousness 102

Young, Robert Alexander 18

Scripture Index

Bruce L. Fields (Ph.D., Marquette University) is assistant professor of biblical and systematic theology at Trinity Evangelical Divinity School. His areas of expertise include Philippians and liberation and black theology.